KNOWING THE KNOWER

The Integral Science of Self

Lex Neale

*"In dedication to World Peace,
one heart at a time".*

Integral Publishers
Tucson, AZ

Integral Publishers
4845E. 2nd St..
Tucson, AZ 85711

Cover design by QTPunque.

All images are author originals or used with permission.

ISBN: 978-1-4951-5911-4

Contents

INTRODUCTION

W E HAVE ARRIVED at an amazing confluence of experience in our evolution: As science approaches its holy grail of a Unified Field of Energy, human awareness is also approaching the Holy Grail of a Unified Self. The scientific proof of a relative truth equating Energy with Mass resulted in a nuclear fireball, which its creator Robert Oppenheimer described as "*a Light brighter than a thousand suns*". He was quoting from an ancient scripture, The Bhagavad Gita, which indeed describes the experiential proof of an Absolute Truth equating Energy with Consciousness that resulted in an explosion of inner Light.

The wreckage we wreak in our evolution from the rational to the trans-rational mind is the result of our landscape shifting from a paradigm to a paradox – from "old concepts no longer apply" to "concepts no longer apply". Toto, we are no longer in Kansas. Similarly when science, from *scious* meaning "knowing", evolves from the practice of rational proofs to the practice of trans-rational proofs, neither do we remain in Kansas either. Trans-rational science, as objectively knowing new fields such as Quantum Consciousness, becomes subjective trans-rational Con-*sciousness*. Outer knowing becomes integral with inner knowing. The moment we equate science with consciousness, we ourselves become the experiment and the proof. Socrates defined the ultimate Science when he allegedly inscribed on the Oracle at Delphi: "Know your Self". Ironically the then prototype Democracy made him drink hemlock for that!

Another way of phrasing Socrates' inscription is "Know the Knower". We know very well that part of our knowing self who observes, opines, evaluates, interprets, judges, justifies, appreciates, and so on. And sometimes will it ever shut up! But whom we rarely see of our Self is the part that is in the background, peacefully witnessing, in awe, beyond words, such as when we are in a state of pure being, even euphoric, as when transported by an experience of utter beauty. In that moment we are closer to our Self as the Knower than we have ever been. In this book we embark on a journey, like a scientific quest, to understand who and what our Knower is.

At our present level of play, we as human beings are becoming more aware that we occupy an Enlightenment vehicle, which has the capacity to consciously evolve our Knowing to a non-dual stage of infinite Knowledge. Our individual Enlightenment, far from being some far-flung idea or ideal, is the one immanent reality of our life in this lifetime. Even in this very life we have now, as our individual being evolves to embrace our Universal Being, our awareness can expand through the Spectrum of Consciousness to embrace the non-dual perspective – that the entire Kosmos is our vehicle, our embodiment, our manifestation.

We are at a point in our exponentially accelerating evolution where all of our knowledge is converging into an integral view of the Kosmos - a theory and practice of everything, embracing all sciences, religions, philosophies and systems of governance. Nothing and Nobody are excluded. As a result, a cosmological model is indeed emerging to describe this integral fact. The first real signs of it happened in the 1920's.

Perhaps the single most profound scientific discovery of the 20th Century was that of Non-local reality. Non-local means energy existing in a non-physical state and **not** conforming to Newtonian or Einsteinian laws. A contemporary of Einstein, Werner Heisenberg, introduced scientists to this non-conformist behavior with his Uncertainty Principle in 1927, which linked the indeterminacy of energy to the experimenter's own consciousness. Einstein famously retaliated with "God does not play dice". Out of the resulting controversy emerged the field of Quantum Physics, shortly followed by the field of Quantum Consciousness. "Consciousness", even now a taboo word in empirical science, suddenly became a key word.

Key words like "consciousness", "mind" and "energy" now need to be redefined etymologically to play their new definitive roles in the emerging fields of consciousness research. In this book I propose a Meta-Theory of Integral Relativity, wherein the terms Consciousness and Mind are no longer used synonymously, but are differentiated as an integral Energy continuum. Integral Relativity predicts that the observer and observed in Heisenberg's Uncertainty Principle are a mutually inclusive Consciousness/Mind/Energy continuum, which expands as an evolving holarchy of knower and known all the way to a Supreme Knower of a Supreme Knowledge.

The differentiation of Consciousness, Mind and Energy is made via a new model that combines with two similar prominent models: Firstly with aspects of the Complex Eight-Dimensional Model of Minkowsky Space (CEDMS), where Minkowky differentiated the four dimensions of Physical Space from four dimensions of "Super-space"; and secondly with aspects of Ken Wilber's Integral Model discussed in Chapter 3, which differentiates four dimensions of Kosmic existence as Four Quadrants. The term "Integral Relativity" as used in Wilber's Integral Theory means taking an All Quadrants, All Levels (AQAL) view of physical existence, or locality; whereas the "Integral Relativity" proposed here integrates an additional Four Quadrants of non-local (non-physical) perspectives, totaling **Eight Fundamental Perspectives** of reality.

In the course of this book, we extend Wilber's Four Quadrants, or AQAL Square, to the Eight Quadrants (or Octants) of the AQAL Cube. The added dimension of a third axis differentiates the Four Quadrants of physical existence (Wilber's model) from Four correlated Quadrants of non-physical existence. But rather than being merely Minkowsky's "Super-space", or the "Non-locality" as defined by Quantum Field Theory, this added Domain of existence also embraces the "Subtle existence" of the Ancient Traditions: the Domain of our Soul, as a Subtle Consciousness monad, with its Subtle Body and Subtle Realms of existence, including after-death existence.

In other words, the Eight Fundamental Perspectives are far from new. We explore several ancient cosmologies incorporating the

Eight Fundamental Perspectives, some of which were introduced by known Enlightenment Teachers to demonstrate how macrocosmic unfolding goes hand in hand with the microcosmic unfolding of the individual awareness. And that paradigm remains unchanged. But what is changing is how the "givens" of non-physical existence, or Metaphysics, are being redefined as experiential realities. For example, many ancient "cultural givens" subjectively underscoring our Eight Fundamental Perspectives, as a Consciousness/Energy continuum, are now being objectively evaluated in Consciousness/Energy research. Quantum physicists such as Amit Goswamy and Nassim Haramein, equate this Consciousness/Energy continuum with recurring fractal patterns of octaves in structural unfolding at the most fundamental levels of energy. The implication being pursued by them, and notable others such as Ervin Laszlo, is that Consciousness is at the root of quantum physical manifestation. For scientists, this is a radical claim, but not irrational.

Ervin Laszlo (2006) in his *"Rationale for an Integral Theory of Everything"* said that for a theory to be truly integral it must offer an **explanation** of everything, not just a **description:**

'An integral TOE identifies the constituents of "every-thing" and states the rules by which the constituents relate to each other so as to form ever more complex things. It identifies the most basic kind of things that exists; the things that generate other things without being generated by them. Then it states the simplest possible set of rules - algorithms - that explain the emergence of the kind of things we have reason to believe exist. If it succeeds, it will be capable of explaining the origins of every-thing in the real world, together with the kind of relations that prevail among them. By extrapolating into the future, it will also be able to explain the kind of developments that are likely to occur: how the existing things transform their relations to each other in time, and transform themselves in the process".

Accordingly, Integral Relativity (as integrating paradigms) via the proposed AQAL Cube model offers explanations for the differentiation of Non-physical and Physical Energy, and for the subsequent relativity between Consciousness, Mind and Energy. As with any hypothesis, Integral Relativity does not provide proofs but explanatory and experiential predictions of proofs. This particularly applies to validating the Enlightenment process as the experiential birthright of any human being.

"Knowing the Knower" is therefore a scientifically based primer for an Integral Science of Self. However, rather than describing the Enlightenment process itself, which has been more than adequately covered by the Ancient Traditions and Metaphysics, we explain here the kosmological basis of Energy, Consciousness, Life and Mind as the experiential underpinnings of Enlightenment. What is Consciousness? What is Energy? What is Life? What is Mind? What is Matter? How do they all come together as a human being capable of experiencing what can only be described as the Absolute Truth of who we really are? Until recently all these questions were considered best left unanswered, as a "Divine Mystery"; but the beauty of this time is that it is Apocalyptic, in the etymological sense that ALL is being "unveiled" and revealed to the All. This is the Information Age. The empirical and experiential proof of phenomena are at last being allowed to proceed hand in hand, resulting in a grand unification of subjective and objective disciplines.

Sri Aurobindo in his Integral Idealism philosophy. said that experiential proof elevates mere philosophy to wisdom. Socrates said "Know your Self", elevating mere science to *Science*, as in "To Know" the Truth of who we really are.

Chapter One

THE QUESTION
OF TRUTH

T HE QUEST FOR the Truth of who we really are is to fulfill an innate evolutionary imperative, to quench an innate thirst for true
peace, for true wholeness. We were born with that imperative,
that need, but the life we actually end up living is a never-ending
search for what we think will bring us satisfaction. We will spend our
whole life grasping whatever substitute we can find to fill that empty
hole; but until we get it right, until we correctly interpret and identify
with that need, our thirst for true fulfillment continues to grow. Life
relentlessly seeks its own true nature until it eventually finds it, even
as a raindrop eventually finds the ocean.

Then what is the nature of Truth? Wars are fought over truth - my
truth against yours. These relative truths are our many points of view,
including the truth we call God. There are religious wars, right now,
all over the planet: Protestants versus Catholics, Christians versus
Jews and Moslems, Jews versus Moslems, Moslems versus Hindus.

Even the search for objective truths reflects our deeper need
for subjective meaning and identity: gender identities, personality
types, family clans, ethnic identities, sociopolitical affiliations, voca-
tional identities and other rationalizations are all mistaken identities
– through misinterpreting our need for identity on the relative level
rather than the absolute level. The Integral model dealt with in this
book shows how the perception and interpretation of "my truth" is a
very complex matter of relativity, dependent primarily on which of

many perspectives we can take, and our altitude (evolutionary level) of each of those perspectives. Most of the conflict on this planet results from people engaging their different perspectives at different altitudes while unknowingly unable to understand their disparity. Ultimately, all this is resolved when the altitudes of all our perspectives enter the rarified air of the Absolute, in Absolution.

The quest for an Absolute Answer is absurd for many, undermining as it does all our rational interpretations, and finally undermining the rational mind itself. But each attempt we make to answer such hard-wired questioning as "Who am I?" leads us to a deeper layer of the question.

First we need to question our definitions before we can establish some truthful basis for Truth. In Greek, "Truth" is a negative: *Alithia*, meaning "Not-forgotten". From *Lithia*, "forgotten", comes the name of the River Lethe, the River of Forgetting, which is crossed by departing Souls. So to understand this definition we have to know what we must "not forget". But implied is that we have already forgotten it, and live in a state of Lithia, amnesia, sleep, unconsciousness, dreams, illusion, ignorance, deception, lies. And to rise out of this state we have to remember, or to wake up to the state of "not-forgetting". To "re-member" means piecing our fragmentation back together. This in Greek is *Eirene*, meaning *Wholeness*, and is their word for *Peace*. So when we "re-member" that Wholeness, that "not-forgotten" Truth, we are in Peace.

Somehow, to forget, Lithia, is in our very nature – a part of the package of being born here. Lithia also means "like stone", as if to forget is to become like stone – inert, heavy and lethargic. If *Alithia* is the Whole Truth, as undifferentiated Consciousness, then Lithia is our material separation from that Consciousness. Material separation is a split, a fragmentation, from being wholly in Peace to being in pieces.

The more materialized Consciousness and Energy become, the more unstable they become. This Physical Universe is a testament of instability, of violent creations and dissolutions in ever tightening cycles. Similarly, the more materialized our focus, the more unstable and psychotic we become. "Material stability" is an oxymoron, guaranteed to shred all our material ambitions and attachments. How much pain is generated through our longing for material stability, for enduring relationships, for a long and healthy life? But being in this world is really like playing in a sandpit, making sand castles that were never meant to last. And yet in a sandpit we also learn to interact, make friends, laugh, learn to love, and grow. Our individual evolving Consciousness is what endures when we leave this world.

To remember that Consciousness, to get our memory back, to wake up from amnesia, we are talking about recovering from a lapse in Consciousness. This "not-forgetting" Truth is therefore a state of Consciousness, which is both "never-forgetting" and "always remembering". For the Greeks, this level of Consciousness is the Memory of the entire Kosmos. If our Soul, according to the ancient Greeks, drowns in the River Lethe on our physical death, it is later physically reborn in amnesia, without memory of previous lives. For a departing Soul to keep hold of that Memory in *Anamnesia*, or in that Truth, it must have the spiritual means to pay for a "ferry" across the River and so keep its unbroken continuity of Consciousness.

This is not just according to the ancient Greeks. Here is a supposed direct quote from Buddha, taken from the most ancient Buddhist text called the *Pali Canon* (palicanon.org), which is a collection of Buddha's discourses recorded as he spoke by his close disciples:

There are four conditions of the embryo into the womb. Bretheren, in this world, one cometh into existence in the mother's womb without knowing. This is the first. Bretheren, one cometh into existence in the mother's womb knowingly, remaineth in it without knowing, and cometh out of it without knowing. This is the second. Bretheren, in this world, one cometh into existence in the mother's womb knowingly, remaineth in it knowingly, and cometh out of it without knowing. This is the third. Bretheren, in this world, one cometh into existence in the mother's womb knowingly, remaineth in it knowingly, and cometh out from it knowingly. This is the fourth.

One might surmise that Jesus meant that state of "not forgetting" when he said "This Truth shall set you free!" Truth, or the liberation of Consciousness, is the sword upheld by Liberty in her right hand; a sword, because Pure Consciousness like pure steel has the sharpness to cut away all that is not true, which is illusion. In her left hand is a pair of scales for weighing that gross materialized consciousness of non-Truth embedded in our Soul. This is what was meant by the weighing of Souls by the Lords of the Dead, as portrayed by many past civilizations. The Souls were weighed against the lightness of a feather to qualify for entry into divine Consciousness.

Another famous example of such a sword is King Arthur's Excaliber. This sword of kingship symbolized the right to rule through being the ruler over one's own Consciousness. In Arthur's case, he fulfilled that right in being able to pull the sword (Consciousness) from the stone (ignorance). In fact, I realized that "Excaliber" could not have been the name of the sword, because it was the Latin inscription on the stone holding the sword: EX CALLE LIBER, meaning *"Free from the stone"*, as a challenge to all-comers. To be able to free the embedded sword was by uttering its secret name, which was "breathed under the breath" as the sword was pulled.

The name of the sword was *"Veritas"*, the Latin for Truth, not a mere name but the not- to-be-forgotten Name of Consciousness itself. *A Varus*, or "in Truth", means *"Awareness"*. The remembering, therefore, is to stay in breath awareness; the message being that our consciousness of breath (*spira* in Latin) leads to *Spirit* Consciousness.

The Quest for Truth in this context is therefore in our aspiring from our amnesia-prone material identity as Ego towards an all-remembering level of spirit identity as Soul. Carlos Castaneda's books describe his very same quest in great detail. In *The Eagle's Gift* he explains how the Yaqui sorcerer, in becoming a Nagual (meaning "Free Soul"), learns to expand his awareness into Eagle Consciousness; so that when he dies his awareness becomes the Eagle's awareness instead of it being consumed as the Eagle's food. This is to say that the state of the Soul's amnesia results from being consumed by the experience of death.

For this reason, the *Tibetan Book of the Dead* is read to the deceased for 49 days in attempt to keep the Soul awake and remembering of continuous Consciousness, after which time it is ready to consciously choose its next incarnation into a more enlightened family. The *Tibetan Book of the Dead* describes an after-death journey whereby we identify our next incarnation. On physical death our Consciousness is released like a bouncing ball. The first bounce is the highest, when we can merge directly back into the Source Consciousness in post-mortem Enlightenment. But if we cannot let go into that vast Beauty, because of gross elements or karmas in our psyche we still cling to, we recoil from the Light of our own radiance and fall into the second bounce. The second bounce is not so high, but nevertheless high enough that we can still potentially let go. Otherwise, if we can still identify with the lesser Light of our higher nature, we can at least land a good rebirth that may lead us to Enlightenment. But if we recoil from our lesser Light because of our heavier karmas, the third bounce can still land us a human incarnation, but of lesser Enlightenment potential. A fourth bounce lands us lesser incarnations for the purpose of resolving those karmas.

Our need for our true identity is so hard-wired into us that most children by four years old are asking "Who am I really? Where do I come from?" This inborn spiritual intelligence of a child then becomes undermined and obscured by the answers from its spiritually unintelligent parents, and its journey through this Underworld begins.

Joseph Campbell examined this in *The Hero of a Thousand Faces* and elucidated the mythographic cycle of the heroic quest for true identity. The hero/heroine searches for a hidden or lost Treasure, or Name, or Key, or Word of Power and so on, the finding of which will lift a curse, a tyranny, a spell, a sickness, a sleep. The hero/heroine by definition is the one who alone finds the courage, often without choice, to embark on such a Quest; which means leaving behind and letting go of the security of our mundane self for the terrifying unknown of the True Self, and then return with the Answer intact.

So our journey through this underworld of our life is the quest for our own true nature. Each birth in a human body is a repeat shot at this process, of crawling out of the un-self-awareness or un-consciousness of our babyhood into ego self-awareness. And then, from getting involved into ego structures to getting evolved back out of them, this process of awakening self-awareness leads us to keep questioning the truth of our identity. In other words, our ego structures are in fact a pre-requisite in the evolution of our identity.

We are born unable to differentiate the boundary between our inside and outside, unable to distinguish between our sense of self and the world out there. As a baby our inner senses and emotions registered the outside world of milk, diaper changes and loving attention as a fused, undifferentiated inner-outer experience. However, in this fused state we learned to differentiate between pleasant and unpleasant experiences - milk and no-milk; diaper change and diaper rash. So began our path to differentiated cognition. Biting our finger instead of the bottle was a fast-track to identifying the boundaries of our body as a separate and primal ego self. Then in our earliest memory formations we learned to anticipate pleasure and pain when we saw the milk coming or not coming, and we cooed or screamed accordingly.

This developing separate sense of self, as our basic ego structure, comes with a sense of primal loss and estrangement from our fused oneness of being with womb-mother. It is an un-namable sense of loss, which will haunt us throughout our life at the core of our ego structure. We learn through survival instincts that the world out there is undependable, not to be trusted. After a few minutes of screaming and there is still no milk or diapers, our very survival is at stake and we go into a red alert which we never quite get over. Worse, this reactivity button will get pressed again and again until an innate sense of anxiety becomes the next ghost to haunt the core of our ego structure. Now we are firm believers in a sense of separation and insecurity, which forms the basis of our belief in the duality of our subjective/objective self-awareness.

Then comes the one factor that could have prevented our loss of sainthood altogether, which is enlightened parenting. As we learned to objectively differentiate our parents from all our other insecurities, did they reflect back to us unconditional love and other aspects of our true Being? Because we become our parents, for better or worse, they who teach us that we must find our purpose somewhere out there in the world, rather than somewhere inside our own being.

The above three stages of our "Fall" from our immortal Being into mortality are: Our primal sense of loss, estrangement and emptiness, which we experience as **inertia**; our primal craving for material substitutes to compensate for our inner loss, which we experience as **desire**; and our primal sense of separation, anxiety and insecurity over our loss, which we experience as **fear**. Inertia, desire and fear are the threefold dynamic of our ego identity. In the center of the Buddhist Wheel of Existence is a pig chasing a rooster chasing a rabbit.

To escape this self-perpetuating cycle of ignorance we must first understand the problem: Our need to awaken into greater self-awareness; our need to become conscious of what we are as yet unconscious. Our evolutionary quest through this labyrinthine world is for greater awareness, which leads ultimately to the Answer – called Enlightenment. It is like a game where we are a pawn on a chessboard striving against great odds towards becoming a Queen. An ancient Hindu board game called *Lila* ("the Game") is the progenitor of Snakes-and-Ladders – where by the roll of dice the player progresses along a path beset by good and bad fortune. To land on a ladder propels the player towards the destination – Enlightenment; but landing on a snake the player plummets down towards the beginning. *Lila* maps out the main pitfalls we face in our evolutionary journey towards Enlightenment.

In the Hindu religion there is a word, which playfully describes the entire Kosmic realm of manifestation: *Mahalila*, which means the "Great Game" played between the Creator and we sentient Creatures. The Game seems to be about our getting lost when we enter, in innocence, an unexpectedly vast arena called The Kosmos; and then about our getting found again – a bit like Hide-and-seek. And like Hide-and-seek, we tend to hide a little too well in this labyrinthine forest we so love to play in; and we wait, and it starts getting dark, and nobody comes, and we start to worry, and we call, and somebody comes to take us home. End of Game. Whew!

Were it only that simple, because it seems to take a long time on the Kosmic timescale before we do start to worry, and even longer before we get it together to call. We forget we were playing Mahalila. This is the truly getting lost part, which Gautama Buddha described as Suffering. And the getting found part - this Buddha termed The End Of Suffering, which is the Dharma – meaning "the Truth".

Ironically, what we usually consider to be our "suffering" are the obvious outer causes, like hunger, poverty, disease, war, corruption, bad neighbors, lousy job, rotten marriage, old age. But the Buddha's message was more subtle – that our individual suffering is within, and can exist even in abundance, health, absence of war and corruption, kind neighbors, youth. As an Enlightenment teacher he was saying the cause of suffering is our own individual ignorance of the Truth within our being, and the end of suffering is to know that Truth within our being. So, if we want peace in our own life, we need to find our inner Peace as a state of inner Wholeness. And if we want peace in the world, we need to first find that Peace within our own self, even if we live in Gaza. And if we want peace in Gaza, it will come to pass when all the people in Gaza find their own inner Peace.

The title of this book *Knowing the Knower* self-proclaims its message, about experiencing our own True Self, with no mention of "Enlightenment". It is unfortunate that the concept of Enlightenment is entangled with religious agendas, especially Buddhism, Taoism and Hinduism, and that the very idea of pursuing the possibility of our own Enlightenment therefore means we have to tangle with one or more of those religious agendas. Thankfully, Buddha was no Buddhist, Lao Tzu was no Taoist, and Krishna was no Hindu, and we can be as conceptually free as they were when they found their True Selves.

So the agenda of this book avoids religious and spiritual concepts as much as possible, and does not attempt to wade through comparative religion and philosophy to "prove" the concept of Enlightenment. Rather, the author tends to go in the opposite direction towards the pragmatics of science, where you wouldn't be seen dead with the words "Consciousness" or "Enlightenment" in your publications!

And yet that drop of awareness doggedly returning to the Ocean of Existence is already trickling its way through the scientific landscape. The discoveries now being made in Quantum Physics and Biology, Integral and Transpersonal Psychology, Cosmology and even Fourier Mathematics show that we are all connected and inseparable in and as an Ocean of Energy! The myriad forms surrounding us are transient waves on its surface. In this book we try to show how our world is awakening to greater empirical Truth, inside and outside, in a glorious symphony of revelation. The tortuous historical process of the emancipation of slaves, of children, of women, of blacks, of gays, is also a metaphor for our long and rocky road leading to the emancipation of Consciousness. At the end of that road our true Armageddon awaits us in "the Unveiling" of our Truth.

In India there is an ancient definition of Truth: *Sat Chit Anand* – meaning "*Truth* is Bliss Consciousness". So now we take a closer look at Truth in terms of an unfolding Consciousness, and Consciousness in terms of an unfolding Kosmos, and Kosmos in terms of an unfolding Life. In the Hindu Kosmos of Mahalila, as in the game Lila, our Life unfolds as a fundamental polarity: we are both sliding down the Snakes of our base desires and fears into *gross materiality* and climbing up Ladders of our aspirations into our *subtle spiritual being*. The paradox is that our material and spiritual natures are co-dependent, co-arising. The teachers of Enlightenment have said throughout history that the means to realizing our radiant Truth is to be found in this material world and in this physical form. And once realizing this, our eyes are opened to the beauty and goodness of this world for what it truly is, and we become like a lotus floating in the sun, while rooted deep in the mud.

Chapter Two

THE IDEALIST KOSMOLOGY OF POLARITY

T HE PARADOX OF our being in this world, but not of it, is born of the same paradox as knowing "Heaven on Earth". The paradox is an apparent duality, a polarity, a separation *without* which there would be no Heaven or Earth in the first place; but *with* which we come to realize that our tortuous sense of separation, so explicit in duality, has an implicit resolution – in knowing our non-duality, our floating in the sun while rooted in the mud. This is the Bliss Consciousness of having our cake and eating it too. Our *Mahalila*. Our Creator at play in Creation.

The Hindu Vedanta cosmology is perhaps the most ancient and the most profound in its telling the story of our Physical, Subtle and Causal existence and awareness. As an Idealist kosmology it transcends and includes the Materialist view – that this physical universe is the be-all and end-all. Rather, it describes our Subtle existence as embedded in, and embodied by, our Physical existence. This polarity view is very much supported by evidence in Quantum Physics, which we deal with in the next chapter. But who better to introduce it here than the Quantum physicist Amit Goswami (1995) in his book *The Self-Aware Universe*:

> *In the Vedanta literature of India, the Sanskrit word "nama" is used to denote transcendent archetypes, and "rupa" signifies their imma-nent form. Beyond "nama" and "rupa" shines the light of Brahman,*

the universal consciousness, the one without a second, the ground of all being...

Perhaps the Taoist symbol of yin and yang is more generally familiar than are the Indian symbols. The light yang, regarded as the male symbol, defines the transcendent realm, and the dark yin, regarded as the female symbol, defines the immanent. "That which lets now the dark, now the light appear is the Tao", the one that transcends its complementary manifestations... In all these descriptions, note that the one consciousness is said to come to us through complementary manifestations: ideas and forms, nama and rupa, Sambhogakaya and Nirmanakaya, yang and yin, heaven and earth. This complementary description is an important facet of idealist philosophy.

In other words, Goswami asserts that the Subtle (*Sambhogakaya*) and Concrete (*Nirmanakaya*) Domains co-exist as two poles of manifestation from the One Un-manifest; and as a polarity they correlate with each other, and therefore co-manifest and co-evolve as two co-equal Domains. He goes on to say that "Manas", etymologically as Mind, is our field of reference within, where our **Subtle Consciousness monad-as-experiencer** (*Vijnanamaya*) identifies our **Concrete Mind-as-experience** (*Manamaya*). This is a key claim, and one that profoundly expands the Integral model of Concrete or Physical existence, discussed in the next chapter; in that our Subtle Consciousness/Soul (*Vijnanamaya/Sambhogakaya*) and our correlated Concrete Mind/Body (*Manamaya/Nirmanakaya*) both co-exist and co-evolve through a spectrum of awareness.

This same bipolarity has been depicted throughout world cultural history in such cosmograms as the Solomon's Seal (Jewish), the Yang-Yin (Chinese), the Hunab Ku (Mayan), the Yab Yum (Tibetan), and the Sri Yantra (Hindu). Throughout history the cultures of the world have consistently discussed human awareness as an interaction between these polarities as two Domains or Fields of awareness: Between Gross Life and Subtle Consciousness, or *Ming* and *Hsing* (Chinese), *Soma* and *Psyche* (Greek), *Briah* and *Atziluth* (Jewish), *Tonal* and *Nagual* (Mayan), *Jivan* and *Atman* (Hindu), *Nirmanakaya* and *Sambhogakaya* (Buddhist), Body-mind and Soul (Christian), and Earth and Moon (Alchemy). With each pair, the former is the incarnate vehicle of the latter. And in both is their Causal Source respectively – in T*ao, Pneuma, Ain Sof, Tonacatecuhtli, Brahman, Dharmakaya*, Spirit, and Sun.

The Vedantic school describes the continuum between Body, Mind, Consciousness and Witness as Koshas, or "sheathes" of awareness, unfolding together through the awareness spectrum, via the Witness at the Causal core, shown in Fig. 1.

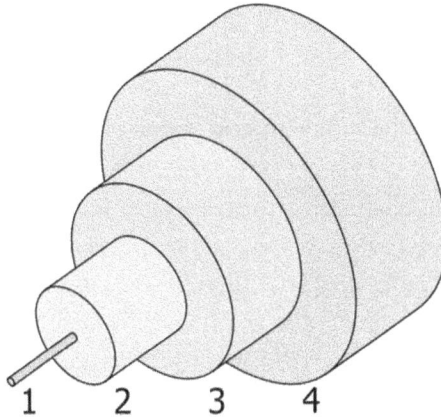

Figure 1. Causal (1), Subtle (2) and Gross Sheathes (3&4)
1. Causal Core as **Witness** (*Anandamaya Kosha*). **2.** Subtle Sheath as **Consciousness** (*Vijnanamaya Kosha*). **3.** Gross Sheath as **Mind** (*Manamaya Kosha*).
4. Gross Sheath as **Body** (*Annamaya Kosha*).

The Body and Mind awareness (*Annamaya* and *Manamaya*) are of the Gross Domain, or *Nirmanakaya*. Conscious awareness (*Vijnanamaya*) is of the Subtle Domain, or *Sambhogakaya*. Witness awareness (*Anandamaya*) is of the Causal Domain, or *Dharmakaya*. Even "within" the Witness is the One Knower (*Brahman*) of the Non-Dual Domain, or *Svabhavikakaya*.

In the Vedantic and other Idealist models, the correlation between Subtle and Gross existence would look like two correlated spectrums, shown in Figure 2.

SUBTLE DOMAIN AND CONSCIOUSNESS (*Sambhogakaya and Vijnanamaya*):

SUBTLE CONSCIOUSNESS SPECTRUM - Consciousness as Levels of Subtle Identity

SUBTLE ENERGY STRUCTURES - Subtle Identification with Bodies and Realms

<   Ego / Low   > <   Soul / High   > < Witness >

RED   to   GREEN   BLUE   to   INDIGO   VIOLET

<   Gross Mind / Simple   > <   Subtle Mind / Complex   > < Causal Mind >

GROSS DOMAIN AND MIND (*Nirmanakaya and Manamaya*):

GROSS MIND SPECTRUM - Mind as Levels of correlated Cognitive Identity

GROSS ENERGY STRUCTURES - Gross Identification with Bodies and Realms

Figure 2: Subtle and Gross Correlated Spectrums

It is as if to say that the Subtle and Concrete spectrums are like Higher and Lower Frequency Bands respectively, like the UHF and VHF Bands of a radio, and that the Causal Domain is like the Super High Frequency carrier wave of the UHF and VHF Bands. Many creation cosmologies describe cosmic manifestation as emerging from a primordial vibration, an unutterable Word, the Om, the Nam or Holy Name of God. Norse myth describes it as a Threefold Shout, which is suggestive of the Shout itself calling forth the Three Domains as Causal, Subtle and Concrete existence.

Looking at Figure 2, we will notice that there is a vertical *Domains hierarchy*, where the **Full Spectrum Gross Domain** below *is correlated* with the **Full Spectrum Subtle Domain** above. The Causal Domain (not shown in Figure 2) transcends and includes the Subtle and Gross Domains. The Causal Domain is that of the full-spectrum Knower, the Witness. In Integral Theory there is the assumption that the Witness is at Ultra Violet, but this is not the case. As full-spectrum, the Witness is the Knower of All Domains and All Levels. Because the Causal Spectrum correlates with the Subtle and Concrete Spectrums, this enables the Knower to omnisciently experience any entity in any Domain at any Level. We discuss this in regards to the standard Integral model in the next chapter.

The ancient and powerful "myth of the given", or cultural assumption, regarding the primary Kosmic Polarity seems to keep re-establishing itself as cultural philosophies evolve, such as from Materialism to Idealism. We would therefore suggest that numerous *contemporary Primary (Vertical) Axis injunctions are completely synonymous with ancient cultural injunctions of the primal Kosmic Polarity*, such as: Implicate and Explicate order, Non-local and Local existence, Disincarnate and Incarnate existence, the "Inside" and "Outside" Domains of Integral Theory (discussed in Chapter 6), the "Real" and "Actual" Selves of Integral Theory, and the "Real" and "Actual" Domains of Critical Realism – where Reality is applied to Causal/Subtle existence as underlying the Actuality of Concrete existence.

In Ken Wilber's *"Towards a Comprehensive Theory of Subtle Energies"* (2012), he says:

> *"In the manifest world, what we call "matter" is not the lowest rung in the great spectrum of existence, but the exterior form of every rung in the great spectrum. Matter is not lower with consciousness higher, but **matter and consciousness are the exterior and interior of every occasion**" [author's bold].*

Exactly the same argument is being made here about the Concrete and Subtle Domains, **where Concrete is not lower with Subtle higher, but** *Concrete and Subtle existence are the "Outside" and "Inside" of every occasion*. In other words, the Subtle is embedded in, and embodied by, the Concrete as a continuum - as Subtle **Consciousness, Bodies and Realms** and Concrete **Mind, Bodies and Realms**.

We now look to the New Science for evidence corroborating these polarities.

Chapter Three

NON-PHYSICAL
AND PHYSICAL POLARITY

M ODERN SCIENCE IS going through another paradigm shift into New Physics, New Biology and New Cosmology. Just as Newton's physical laws propelled humanity out of religious dogma into the Industrial Revolution, and Einstein's Relativity propelled us to outer space, so Max Planck's Quantum Dynamics propelled us out of Kansas into an Oz of "weird science", which even Einstein had trouble coming to terms with.

From the very outset a hundred years ago, the founders of Quantum Mechanics suspected a link between the consciousness of an experimenter/observer and the behavior of the energy being observed. Max Planck, John Wheeler and Werner Heisenberg all saw a quantum link between human awareness and the Divine, as co-creators. An un-sourced quote of Max Planck says:

> *I regard consciousness as fundamental. I regard matter as a derivative from consciousness. We cannot get behind consciousness. Everything that we talk about, everything that we regard as existing, postulates consciousness... There is no matter as such. All matter originates and exists only by virtue of a force. We must assume behind this force is the existence of a conscious and intelligent Mind. This Mind is the matrix of all matter.*

One hundred years later it seems things are coming full circle back to that realization. Quantum Mechanics has established that the Physical Universe condenses into manifestation out of a very dense Quantum Field of unformed Energy, also known as the Zero Point Field. In other words "empty space" is now an oxymoron, because it is like an Ocean of which we fish are completely oblivious. Energy in the Zero Point Field has not yet been subjected to the rules and regulations of the Physical Universe and Space-time; where the speed of light, gravitation and any form of ordered and predictable behavior still do not apply.

In a recent groundbreaking paper, Quantum Physicist Nassim Haramein (2013) announced his discovery that the quantum mass inside a single proton equals the estimated mass of the entire universe! This is weird science, indeed, until one makes the connection: as a wave-vortex, a proton is not separate from all other energy as some isolated "particle"; it only seems separate, just like a wave only seems separate from the ocean it actually is. And if a proton is contiguous with All Energy Everywhere, then it has no individual mass, but a contiguous holographic mass of All Energy Everywhere with **no separation in space or time**.

This is basically a quantum affirmation of "Indra's Net", as described in the Avatamska Sutra of the Mahayanas:

"Far away in the heavenly abode of the great god Indra, there is a wonderful net which has been hung by some cunning artificer in such a manner that it stretches out infinitely in all directions. In accordance with the extravagant tastes of deities, the artificer has hung a single glittering jewel in each "eye" of the net, and since the net itself is infinite in dimension, the jewels are infinite in number. There hang the jewels, glittering "like" stars in the first magnitude, a wonderful sight to behold. If we now arbitrarily select one of these jewels for inspection and look closely at it, we will discover that in its polished surface there are reflected all the other jewels in the net, infinite in number. Not only that, but each of the jewels reflected in this one jewel is also reflecting all the other jewels, so that there is an infinite reflecting process occurring."

An identical "heavenly artifice" is the "Dreamcatcher" web spun by Native American creatrix Spider Woman, which is a web of conscious interconnectivity between all peoples. In it the consciousness of every individual is suspended like a jewel.

The quantum implications of a contiguous holographic web of Energy / Consciousness are world changing. If we could vibrate at that fundamental level of Energy, would we also find ourselves in a state of "omnipresence"? And if at that level, where a conscious intention induces Einstein's famous "spooky action at a distance", would we find ourselves in a state of "omnipotence"? Planck's law states that the more fundamental the frequency of Energy vibration, the more information it embraces. If we could vibrate at that fundamental frequency, would we also find ourselves in a state of "omniscience"?

Indeed, there is now overwhelming evidence that the "Ocean" of Energy *is* Aware. In the New Physics, mounting empirical evidence in quantum consciousness research points to a post-post-modern verification of the Vedanta's differentiation between the Subtle and Concrete Domains of existence as timeless non-local Super-space and local Space-time; and where consciousness has access to that non-local Super-space.

The most significant general model being used in quantum physics is the CEDMS - Complex Eight Dimensional Minkowsky Space. Well before Einstein, Minkowsky was the first to add the fourth dimension of time to three-dimensional space. Einstein later adopted that model. Then Minkowsky went a step further, where even Einstein feared to tread, and added to the four physical dimensions an additional four correlated, but hypothetical, dimensions that mapped a correlated hypothetical reality beyond the domain of conventional physics. It was an intuitive leap into a domain that would later become known as Non-local, shown in Figure 3, from K. Renshaw's *Why Quantum Entanglement Works* (2011).

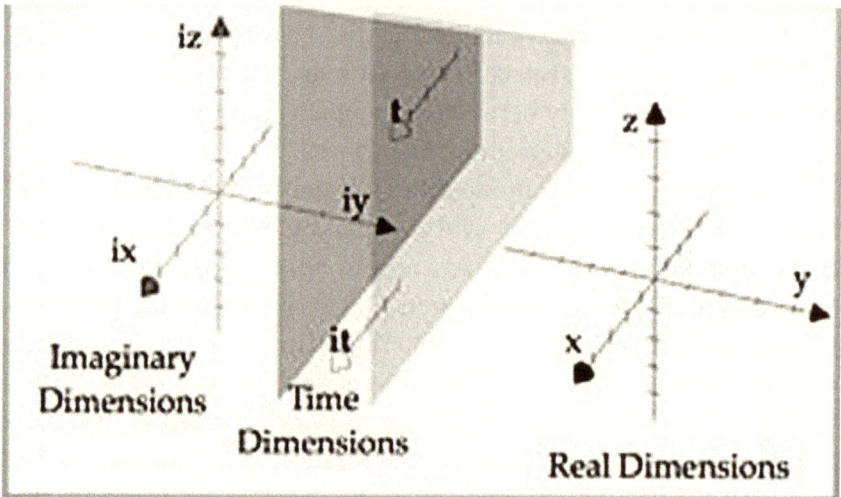

Figure 3. Complex Eight Dimensional Minkowsky Space

The person who adapted the CEDMS model to Quantum Physics was Elizabeth Rauscher (2008), who continues to be its leading advocate. She explains:

> *Events that are remote in four (dimensional) space... are contiguous in the complex eight-space... In this model, space-time events can become contiguous in the complex eight-space, demonstrating that the remoteness of the observer and the observed can become contiguous in the complex eight-space in which causality conditions are preserved and the acquisition of apparent remote information is allowed.*

In other words, a direct connection can exist between local and non-local energy, a condition called entanglement, which can be modeled by CEDMS. The CEDMS model set the stage for a groundbreaking discovery published in *arXiv* by Pusey (2011) and reported in *Nature* a few days later, on November 17th 2011, by Eugenie Reich:

> *Whereas many physicists have generally interpreted the wave function as a statistical tool that reflects our ignorance of the particles being measured, the authors of this paper argue that, instead, it is physically real.*

"Physically real" means that the quantum wave function carries *real encoded information* from non-local or non-physical "Superspace" into physical locality, rather than mere statistical probabilities. This is a prerequisite to be able to model non-local reality, and in effect validates the basis of Quantum Consciousness/Mind as an empirical science.

Planck's Law states that as Energy frequency tends towards infinity, so does its capacity for information. Given that the frequency of Concrete energy increases as it approaches the "infinity" of the Zero Point Field, or the undifferentiated quantum vacuum, the implication is that non-local Superspace could be the repository of **all** the information in the Concrete Spectrum. This is further suggestive of a non-local Field of Consciousness, which Ervin Laszlo (2007) proposes in *"Science and the Akashic Field"* is synonymous with the Universal Mind or Akashic Field. In the Vedantas, the Akasha is the infinite and eternal domain of Kosmic Memory.

In other words, it is likely that Planck's Law will end up validating the Ancient Traditions claim of the Akashic Field, and that the Physical Universe is an open and evolving system, that is supported by, and exchanges information with, an underlying Non-physical reality. The currently held view in cosmological science is that the Physical Universe is "entropic", meaning that as a closed system it is slowing down, "running out of steam". However, it is now becoming apparent that the Physical Universe is embedded in a Subtle Universe, which not only energizes the Physical Universe as a "negentropic" system but is also the Intelligence behind it.

In the field of mathematics, the cutting edge mathematician Mike Hockney says in his ebook *The Mathmos* (2014):

> *Reality is actually straightforward. It comprises two domains: a dimensionless frequency domain outside space and time and a dimensional, material domain inside space and time, the two being linked by Fourier mathematics.*

We go deeper into this in Chapter 12 – "Integral Relativity and the Primary Axis Injunction". Suffice it to say here that while Hockney sees the dimensionless "Super-space" as that of energy mathematics underlying this material domain, Quantum Physics is showing that Hockney's domain of energy mathematics is that of conscious information.

Director of Research at the Institute of Noetic Science, Dr. Dean Radin (2013) does rigorous quantum experiments to demonstrate both the non-locality and locality of a subject's awareness. The inference we can draw from his work is that our quantum consciousness/mind, operating in non-locality at the Zero Point Field of the quantum vacuum, is firmly embedded in the core of this Concrete Physical Universe. Radin has recently published a compendium "*Show Me the Evidence*" (2013) of empirical research from around the world that similarly demonstrates the non-locality of consciousness/mind. Calling this the Psi Field, Radin's experiments are paving the way towards the physics of quantum consciousness/mind.

Quantum physicist Dr Amit Goswamy, in a paper on the quantum basis of Morphic Resonance (2003), compared Rupert Sheldrake's Morphogenic Fields with quantum consciousness/mind. The experiments of Sir Roger Penrose and Dr Stuart Hameroff (1996) are on the same trajectory. Hameroff (2011), in an interview with *EnlightNext* said:

> *You know, most people think that consciousness emerged over eons as a byproduct of random mutations and the inherent complexity of natural selection, but I look at it the other way around. I think a fundamental field of protoconscious experience has been embedded all along – since the big bang – in the Planck scale, and that biology evolved and adapted in order to access it and to maximize the qualities and potentials implicit within it.*

It is becoming apparent that *Concrete full-spectrum Energy*, experientially processed as our *Concrete full-spectrum Mind*, is synonymous with the various "Psi", "Chi", "Morphogenic", "Pranic", "Astral" and "Akashic" Templates that are laid down in unfolding Waves of an individual's evolving Concrete awareness, from proto-mind to Universal Mind. Right there we have entered the arena of a New Science that is empirically validating many ancient sciences from the world's cultural history.

The main impact that these "non-physical energies" are having on conventional science, particularly neuroscience, is the obviation of both the "Qualia Problem" - of how states of experiential awareness are formed; and the "Hard Problem" – of how the brain "generates" its own experiential awareness through upward causation. In fact, it is becoming apparent that the situation in reality could be reversed: that our non-local Consciousness translates its intentions into locality via Mind, which in turn enacts them via the brain as appropriate sensory and physical actions of our body. By analogy, it is not the computer that assembles itself, then writes and installs its own software; but is the programmer (Subtle Consciousness) who creates the software programs (Concrete Mind) that run the computer (Brain) that operates the biomechanics (Body).

This brings us to the Origin of Life question, which is again the Hard Problem as a bigger picture. The conventional scientific approach to the origins of life and consciousness is by upward causation: that evolving organic complexity leads to organic life, which leads to neural complexity and ultimately consciousness. The New Physics paradigm includes downward causation and the involution of Non-local Consciousness as a function of organic complexity. We discuss this in detail in the chapter 10 - "Volution as a Primary Axis Dynamic".

Perhaps the most integral model capable of mapping all these New Physics developments, and which also takes consciousness "all the way down", is Ken Wilber's Four Quadrants Square (1995). This maps existence through Four Fundamental Perspectives (All Quadrants), and through levels of complexity (All Levels) of Gross, Subtle and Causal existence. The AQAL (acronym) Square maps Four Fundamental Perspectives (Quadrants) of existence as Individual Interiors, Individual Exteriors, Collective Interiors and Collective Exteriors, shown in Figure. 4.

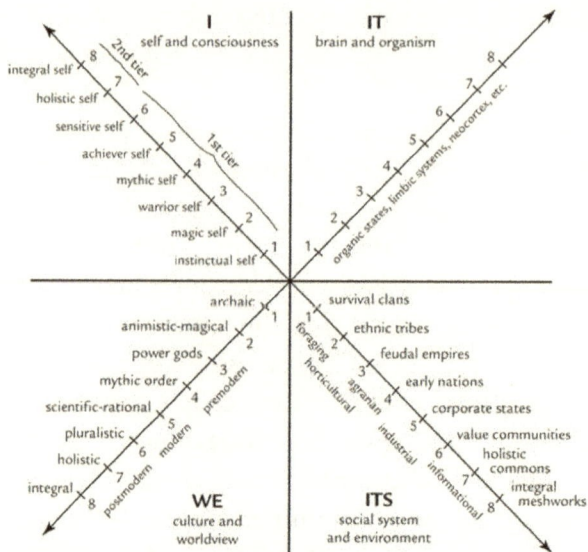

Figure 4. Wilber's "AQAL Square" Four Quadrant Model

From the "Zero Point" in the center of the Quadrants, which is also synonymous with the "Zero Point Field", physical manifestation unfolds simultaneously through four fundamental perspectives. The Individual Interior Quadrant (Upper Left) shows a proto-conscious proto-individual experientially evolving through levels of cognitive awareness, from fundamental sensations to Enlightenment. The Individual Exterior Quadrant (Upper Right) shows the correlated energy structures required to process that evolution through levels of complexity, from fundamental energies to the human form. The Collective Interior Quadrant (Lower Left) shows the correlated interrelationships evolving as worldviews, from fundamental experiential exchange to a compassionate caring for the whole of existence. The Collective Exterior Quadrant (Lower Right) shows correlated collective activity evolving as systems, from the primordial aggregation of energies into galaxies to the harmonious organization of utopian society. However, the AQAL Square is a Concrete Domain *Levels holarchy*, where each Level of evolution embraces and operates with all previous Levels. The Gross, Subtle and Causal Levels in each Quadrant are of correlated physical complexity, and this model therefore cannot map non-physical existence being explored in New Science and New Metaphysics.

The Integral Relativity proposed here is an *All Domains holarchy* of Gross, Subtle and Causal Domains, with a vertical *Primary Axis* that differentiates the *Physical/Gross Domain* from the *Non-Physical/ Subtle Domain* as two co-AQAL Polarities; thus dimensionally expanding Wilber's AQAL Square to an AQAL Cube.

The vertical Primary Axis of the AQAL Cube differentiates an entire AQAL Subtle Domain and Consciousness above (aka *Sambhogakaya* and *Vijnanamaya*) as *Octants 1,3,5,7*; and correlated with an entire AQAL Concrete Domain and Mind below (aka *Nirmanakaya* and *Manamaya*) as *Octants 2,4,6,8*; which totally conforms with Quantum Physics, Vedantic traditions and Idealism. They both are full-spectrum correlates, as shown in Figure 5.

Subtle Quadrants 1,3,5,7

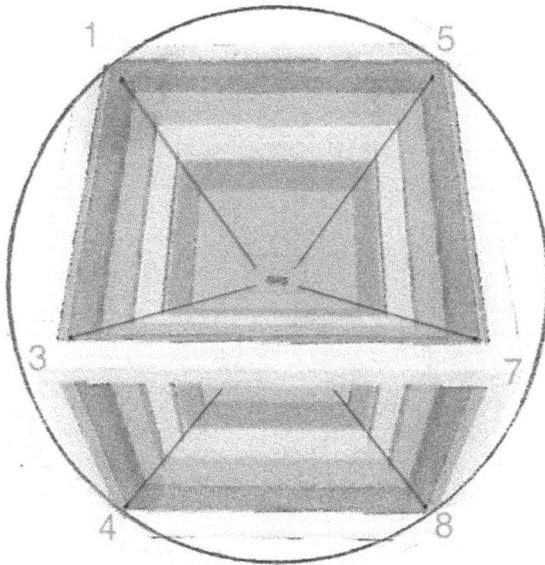

Concrete Quadrants 2,4,6,8

Figure 5. AQAL Cube as correlated Concrete and Subtle Spectrums

The AQAL Cube differentiates the Two Axes of Wilber's Four Quadrants Square (*Interiors-Exteriors* and *Individuals-Collectives*) along a vertical Primary Axis, the poles of which are: AQAL *Concrete (Local)* existence below, as per Wilber's AQAL Square, and the proposed correlated AQAL *Subtle (Non-Local)* existence above. This gives Eight Fundamental Perspectives formed at each corner of the Cube where three faces of the Cube come together as a triplet-codon (Figure 6).

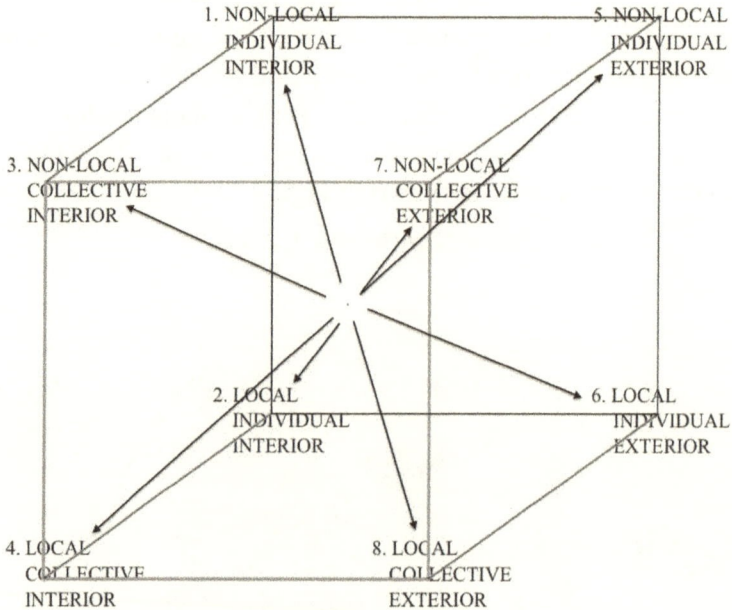

1. NON-LOCAL INDIVIDUAL INTERIOR

5. NON-LOCAL INDIVIDUAL EXTERIOR

3. NON-LOCAL COLLECTIVE INTERIOR

7. NON-LOCAL COLLECTIVE EXTERIOR

2. LOCAL INDIVIDUAL INTERIOR

6. LOCAL INDIVIDUAL EXTERIOR

4. LOCAL COLLECTIVE INTERIOR

8. LOCAL COLLECTIVE EXTERIOR

Figure 6. The AQAL Cube's Eight Perspectives of Non-Locality/Locality

Each face of the Cube therefore yields a tetra-dynamic of perspectives: The Local Quadrants (below) as physical manifestation, the Non-local Quadrants (above) as non-physical manifestation, the Interior Quadrants, Exterior Quadrants, Individuals Quadrants and Collectives Quadrants. These six tetra-dynamics make the AQAL Cube a very powerful tool to analyze the dynamics of cosmic manifestation.

If the AQAL Cube really is a fundamental cosmological model, we would expect to see evidence of it in our cultural history. This is indeed the case, and so before we go any further with the AQAL Cube model, we first look into our cultural history to see how the Cube has had numerous similar reincarnations as a cosmological model, with a vertical Primary Axis and two Horizontal Axes that form a basic Tree of Life.

Chapter Four

THE TREE OF CONSCIOUSNESS AND LIFE

T HE TREE OF Life in all its cultural forms is a perennial archetype representing cosmic manifestation bearing the fruits of Consciousness. Many myths about primordial culture heroes and heroines describe their arduous labors to obtain those fruits of Consciousness. Odin hung for three days on the Tree Yggdrasil before receiving the gift of Celestial Sight; the Buddha became Enlightened after meditating under a sacred Bhodi Tree; the Mayan Time Lords became rulers of the Cosmos after ascending a Kosmic Maize Plant.

The implication is that while our awareness does just grow on trees, we also have to climb for it. One Book described a primordial paradise where grew two Trees: one bearing fruits of eternal Life, and the other bearing the more tempting fruits of Good and Evil – sounding suspiciously like a Tree of Consciousness and a Tree of Mind with its serpent – the latter luring our awareness into the dubious world of sensory experience, for better or worse.

Sure enough, after taking a bite from a sensuous red apple, the primordial couple living in the Garden of Eden found themselves looking equally tasty to each other, and wandered off out of the Garden, which then disappeared into the mists of time. Poor Eve and all women thereafter took the "Fall" for that one! But the subtler message here is that rather than lose our eternal Consciousness to our mortal material Mind, the non-dual trick is to enjoy the fruits of both *without leaving the Garden.*

A Cube of Three Axes is the most ancient cosmological model of the Tree of Kosmic manifestation. The cube, as form expanding along three axes, is the Chinese cosmogram shown in Figure 7. On the vertical axis the single unbroken line above is Heaven (Yang), and the single broken line below is Earth (Yin), as the primordial Patrix and Matrix, by whom are conceived the two horizontal axes of primordial manifestation as their four sons and daughters.

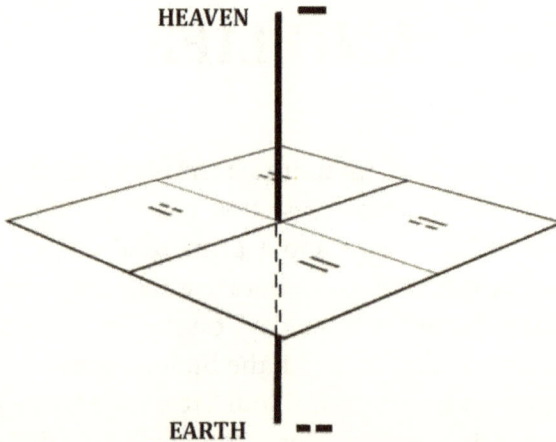

Figure 7. Chinese Tree of Primordial Manifestation

Lao Tzu intoned in the *Tao Te Ching*: "*Out of the One came Two; out of the Two came Three; and out of the Three came Ten Thousand Things.*"

The primordial Tree of Life in Figure 7 shows the four "bigrams" of primordial manifestation as Yang/Yin recombinant permutations emerging from the Primal Axis. The age-old Chinese cosmogram of the primal Yang-Yin polarity is called the *Tai Chi*, meaning "Movement (Yang) of Breath (Yin)". Breath in a creation cosmology is *Spira*, or "Spirit" – Movement of Spirit.

A very similar Mayan cosmogram of the primal polarity is called *Hunab Ku*, meaning "Movement and Measure". Again, on the one hand there is Movement, meaning the Primordial Patrix or Kosmic Father of Time-as-Change; and on the other hand there is Measure, meaning the Matrix or Kosmic Mother of Primordial Space. It is the arena of Primordial Space-Time, wherein the Primordial Kosmos of formless Energy can differentiate in the "Womb" of Primordial Space as form.

The cosmograms in Figure 8 show the dynamic of the Primal Polarity working together, each pole coming through the other, as our involution (Life, dark, feminine, compassion) and our evolution (Consciousness, light, masculine, wisdom).

Figure 8. Tai Chi and Hunab Ku Cosmograms

In all tri-axial Tree of Life creation cosmologies, the vertical axis is the primary Axis Mundi separating "Heaven from Earth", or the Kosmic Patrix from the Kosmic Matrix. All subsequent kosmogonic unfolding through all Levels of polarity differentiation goes according to this same fundamental paradigm, like a steamy tango of love-making. Yes, it takes two to tango. *It is for this reason that the Subtle and Concrete Domains, as polarities, are co-emergent and co-equal,* because they are extensions of the primal co-emergent and co-equal polarity of the Kosmic Patrix and Matrix.

In Figure 9, like a Tree of Life itself, is a vastly over-simplified progression of polarities/dualities that differentiate in the process of Kosmic manifestation, called Involution, and the reversed process of reintegrating those polarities/dualities, called Evolution.

Kosmogenesis is, therefore, a process of differentiating correlated polarities, or dualities, through levels of decreasing frequency in both the Concrete and Subtle Spectrums. Reversed kosmogenesis, as the Enlightenment process, is in reconciling or "remembering" those dualities back through levels of increasing frequency to the

INVOLUTION
Differentiating Polarities

NON-DIFFERENTIATED ENERGY
AS THE ONE KNOWER

Kosmic Patrix   Kosmic Matrix
Supreme Witness   Akashic Mind
                       ATONEMENT

Causal Consciousness   Causal Mind
                       ENLIGHTENMENT

Subtle Consciousness   Higher Mind
                       INTEGRATION OF SOUL

Lower Consciousness   Lower Mind
                       INTEGRATION OF EGO

Proto-consciousness   Proto-mind
                       LIFE

Wave   Particle/Elements
                       UNIFIED FIELD

NON-DIFFERENTIATED ENERGY
AS UNCONSCIOUSNESS

EVOLUTION
Integrating Polarities

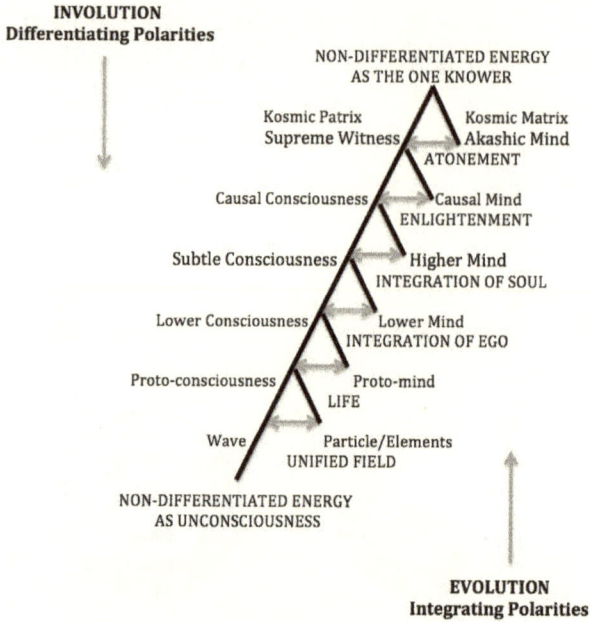

Figure 9: Title: Involution and Evolution

non-dual primordial state. So it comes as no surprise that a kosmo-logical model also serves as an Enlightenment model.

The earliest Tree of Life cosmological model ever conceived was our own human form that the Old Testament says was "made in the Image of God". There is a message here, in that God-as-Kos-mos equates with God-as-human because the human form is planet Earth's one and only Enlightenment vehicle. The story continues that our first form was "made of clay", into which our Maker "breathed" Life. And we're not just talking mouth-to-mouth resuscitation here. We are Spirit beings.

We are a Tree of Life as microcosm, and the Ancient Traditions give attributes to our Three Axes: We stand on a vertical axis. Our head (Up) contains our *Consciousness*, through which we evolve. Our feet (Down) walk the path of *Life*, by which we evolve. Hori-zontally we face our *individual path* Ahead. We leave Behind our *collective origins*. With our Right hand we create our *outer objectives*. With our Left hand we receive our *inner guidance*. Already we have an Integral Model, but more. Our vertical axis is our *Growth*; our ahead/behind axis is our *Direction*; and our right/left axis is our *Balance*. The three axes intersect in our heart, our Within. These three axes form a simple Tree of Life cosmogram with the six directional perspectives in First Person, as in Figure 10.

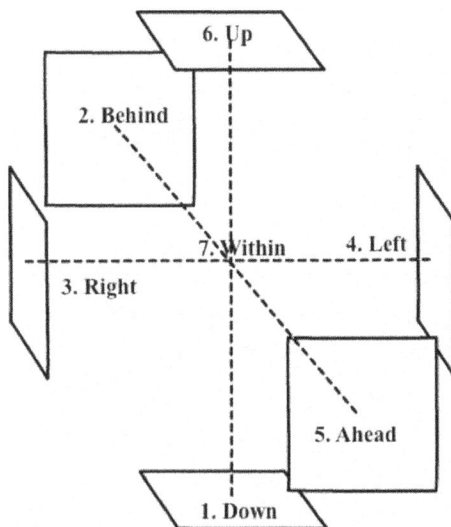

Fig. 10. Six Directional First Person Perspectives

On the Directional axis (ahead/behind), our purpose leads us to the *Truth* of who we are. On the Balance axis (right/left), our endeavors lead us to the *Goodness* of who we are. On the Growth axis (up/down), the evolution of our identity through form leads us to the *Beauty* of who we are. Our Truth is ultimately omniscient, our Goodness is ultimately omnipotent, and our Beauty is ultimately omnipresent.

Joseph Campbell, the iterator-in-chief of the mythological quest, gave a famous one-liner: "Follow your bliss". In India another famous one-liner is "Truth is Bliss-consciousness". So, if following our Truth is synonymous with following our Bliss, Campbell was saying that is the direction, the purpose of our quest. However, the quest itself is beset with trials that are the proof of our worthiness to fulfill the quest; trials that prove our essential Goodness in selfless service when helping a beggar or overcoming a tyrant along the way. And in keeping to our Truth, and in proving our Goodness, we grow in Beauty. Another famous one-liner of the Native Americans is "Walk in Beauty".

Through this Cube of Being (Below) and Knowing (Above) we evolve in six directions as the Six Faces of Spirit. As we individually evolve in this life we pass through Self-identity phases of how we see ourselves as "I" in the center of it all. As a baby, our "I" is a fused experience with mother and milk, known as the Id. When we become materially self-aware, our Self-identity shifts to the Ego. And when we become spiritually self-aware, our Self-identity shifts again to that of Soul-awareness. Ultimately, our "I" shifts to "I AM", our true Self-as-Witness. In Figure 11 we see how our world-view changes as we move through (a) the Id, (b) the Ego, (c) the Soul and (d) the Witness:

(a) Id

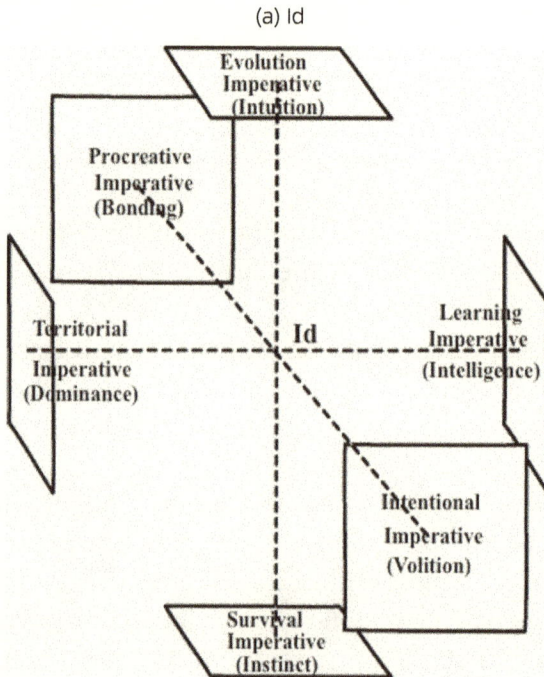

(b) Ego

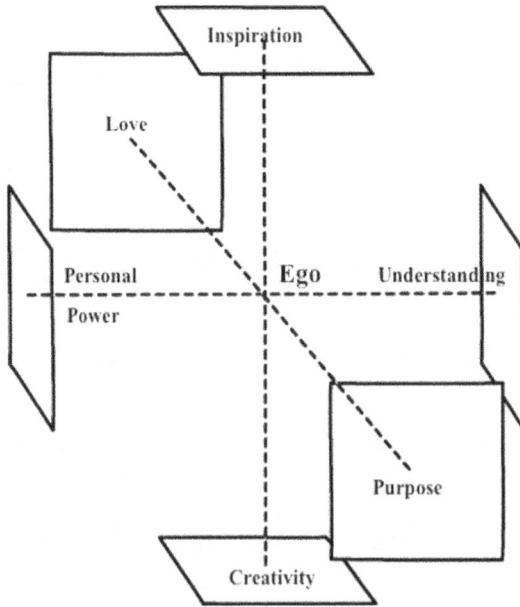

(c) Soul

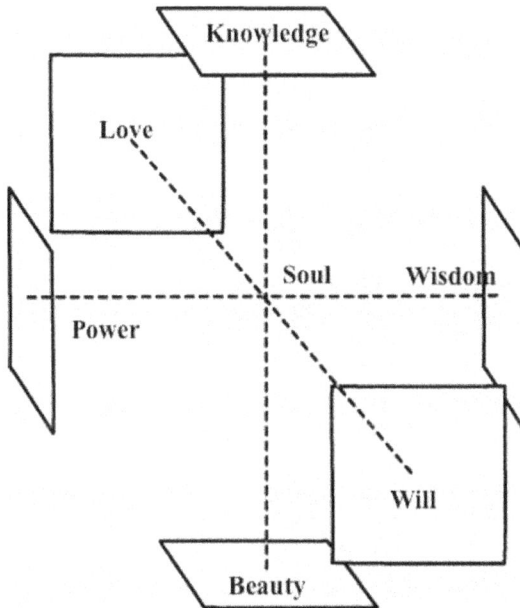

(d) Witness

All - Father

Wisdom of
Essential
Equality

Causal
Witness

All-discriminating
Wisdom

Mirror Wisdom

All - Pervading
Wisdom

All-accomplishing
Wisdom

All - Mother

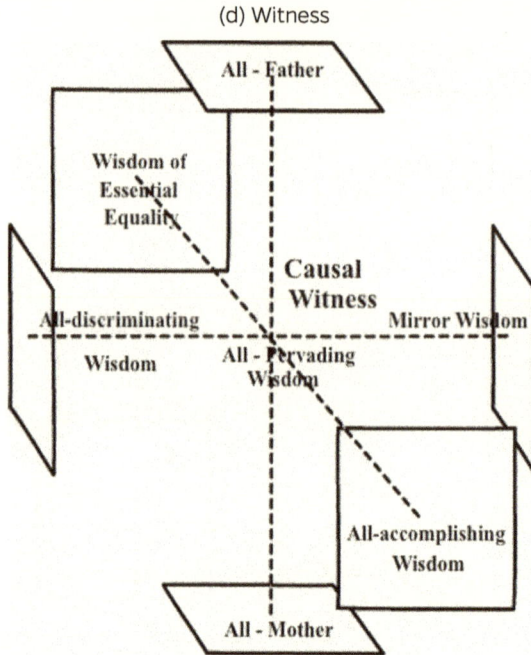

Figure 11. The Six Faces of Spirit through Four Levels

1. *Below* is the foundation on which we build our material Being, our Life, where we manifest the *Beauty* of the Kosmos.

2. *Behind* is the collective womb out of which we emerge, where we inherit the unconditional *Love* of the Kosmos.

3. On the *Right*, through our objectives, we obtain the *Power* of the Kosmos.

4. On the *Left*, through subjectively integrating our experience, we become the *Wisdom* of the Kosmos.

5. *Ahead*, in pursuing our individual truth or purpose, we orient ourselves to the *Will* of the Kosmos.

6. *Above*, through our non-material Consciousness, we are the *Knowledge* of the Kosmos.

7. *Within* we are *Witness* to all this, the *Knower* of the Kosmos.

In the Ancient Traditions, *these are the numbered attributes of the Seven Chakras* from Base to Crown. A very simplified description of the Chakras, as levels of awareness, starts with our *survival awareness* based in the First Chakra. Then comes our *relational awareness*, starting with our family, in the Second Chakra. Soon we are out there in the world providing for our family with *material awareness* and the personal power of our Third Chakra. But as we become more *self-aware* in the Fourth Chakra, we realize our responsibilities embrace a greater whole. From the Fifth Chakra we find our higher purpose or calling in *spiritual awareness*. And we realize that calling in the Sixth Chakra as *illumined awareness*, and *enlightened awareness* in the Crown Chakra.

Which brings us to one of the most ancient cosmological models known the world over – the *Cubic Die*. The author's research revealed it to be a teaching tool for the Enlightenment process through our Direction, Balance and Growth. It shows how the macrocosm as Kosmos and the microcosm of the human being are not-two, and as such is an Enlightenment cosmology demonstrating non-duality.

Like the temple virgin who became abused as a temple prostitute, every cubic die thrown into the green felt arena of fate and fortune, in every casino in the world, carries the same mark of the divine and of divination: All dice carry their spots with the same paired polarities of *1 - 6, 2 - 5 and 3 - 4*, as shown in Figure 12. The miracle is that they have retained this order, unchanged for thousands of years. I have been to museums and examined ancient dice of the Greeks, Romans, Egyptians, Sumerians, Phoenicians, Babylonians, and they are all identical..

Figure 12. The Cubic Die

The spots are arranged as three paired polarities: 1 – 6, 2 – 5, 3 – 4, each adding up to seven. Clearly, seven is the implied completion number at the center of the three intersecting axes. Why?

In cultures worldwide the cube represents the element Earth. Salt, as in "salt of the Earth", is a cubic crystal. In alchemical cosmology, salt represents the *Materia Mater* or material consciousness to be transmuted into spiritual consciousness. So the cubic die represents each of us in our mortal life of material consciousness on this planet, cast as we are into this green arena of fate and fortune, in this crapshoot called Life. And, following the alchemical clue of *Materia Mater*, the aim of the game is to transform our base Mind as Lead, via the Six Chakras, into the Gold of Consciousness: To throw a 7.

I knew there had to be a way, used to be a way, of casting a cubic die to give perfectly *equal odds 1 through 7,* so that the die could divine the cosmology it contains. The mathematicians I knew accused me of dreaming. Sure enough, the solution came to me in a dream in the dead of night, and I momentarily woke up remembering how to do it. Unfortunately, I woke up the next morning clueless, and spent some weeks in limbo until it came back to me – where else but in the bathtub.

To throw 1 through 7 *with equal probability* with a cubic die is accomplished in either two or three throws. The first throw gives a number 1 through 6. The second throw gives either a different number or a double. If a different number, then the first number thrown stands. But if the second throw gives a double, this double potentially stands as a 7, but it must be confirmed with a third throw. The third throw gives either a different number or a triple. If a different number, then the 7 stands. But if the third throw gives a triple, the number of the triple stands. When this enlightenment cosmology was forgotten, so was the means of casting 1 to 7.

Probabilities: 16.6666 per cent for each number 1 through 6 on the first throw. Next, 16.6666 percent for any double (potentially 7) on the second throw. But the second throw then reduces chances of each number 1 through 6 to 100 minus 16.6666, divided by six, which equals 13.8889 per cent.

Error: 16.6666 - 13.8889 = 2.7777 per cent in favor of 7 on the second throw. To eliminate this error a third throw is required, which may result in a triple. Probability of any triple = 2.7777 per cent. This exactly cancels out the above bias in favor of 7.

If we are the Die, then our spots are the Six Faces of Spirit as shown in Figure 11, whose attributes are those of our Seven Chakras shown in Figure 13.

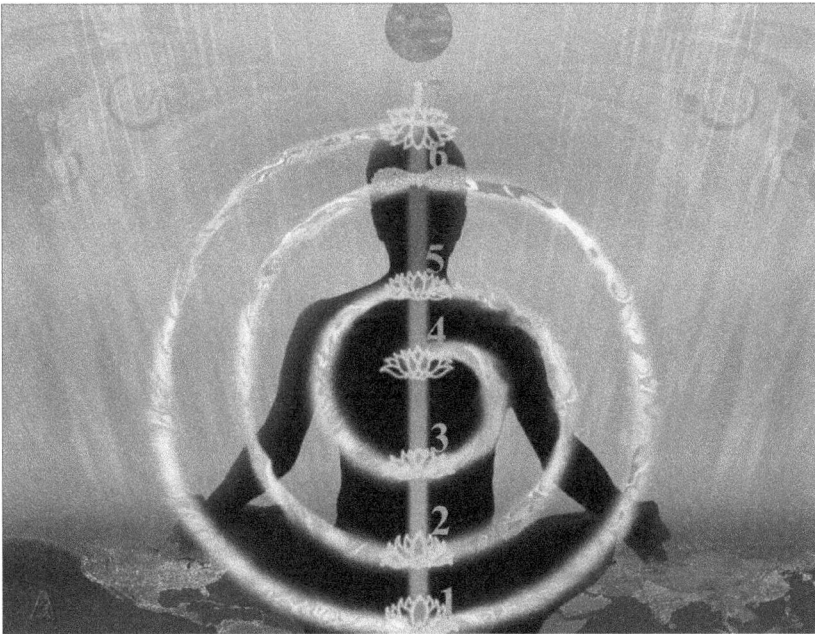

Figure 13. The Seven Chakras Breath Spiral

We are looking at an Enlightenment cosmology based on seven, like the Seven Colors of the Rainbow - Red, Orange, Yellow, Green, Blue, Indigo and Violet - which is a metaphor for Levels of awareness in the Spectrum of Consciousness. Our means of transformation through the Chakras is the Breath Spiral, and Figure 13 shows how *the Breath Spiral forms polarity pairs* between the Chakras that are exactly those of the Cubic Die: *1 - 6, 2 - 5 and 3 - 4*. The way that our breath awareness through the Chakras leads to Spirit awareness is dealt with later.

So far we have considered the Six Faces of Spirit on the Cube. We now consider the Eight Fundamental Perspectives formed at each of the eight corners of the Cube, where three Faces come together, shown in Fig. 6. If our Eight Fundamental Perspectives truly are cosmological archetypes like the Six Faces of Spirit, we would expect to see their evidence both in our biological and cultural history. And again, this is indeed the case.

Chapter Five

THE EIGHT PERSPECTIVES
AS ARCHETYPES

I N CHAPTER 3 we saw how the three axes of the AQAL Cube model form six polarities, and how these in turn form Eight Fundamental Perspectives at the vertices of the Cube. Through the course of this book we follow the Eight Fundamental Perspectives as a cosmological template of polarity differentiation, through all levels of manifestation. This is because they define the fundamental dimensions of an unfolding Kosmos as Energy and Matter, Consciousness and Life.

As the unfolding into form takes place, the density and complexity of form increase. However, the complexity is only apparent because Kosmic unfolding into form adheres to, and progresses by, very **simple** mathematical patterns such as the Fibonacci series, Fourier Transformations and algorithms.

Kosmic unfolding is a correlated evolutionary progression not only through the three facial axes of the cube but also through its four diagonal axes that connect the eight vertices as the Eight Fundamental Perspectives. No surprise therefore that the Eight Fundamental Perspectives have been present as a perennial cultural concept for at least the last several thousand years. However, if they really do form an archetypal template of awareness, we should be able to see how they became operational when Life first began on planet Earth some five or more billion years ago.

A simple organism's awareness of its environment begins through dependably recurring stimuli, by which it learns to regulate its survival behavior. From the orbital motions of the Sun, Moon and Earth come the Solar Seasons, Lunar Months, Sunrise and Moonrise. And from the regularity of these cycles emerges all biorhythmic behaviors: A time to wake and a time to sleep, a time to feast and a time to hibernate, a time to mate and a time to migrate. An organism's biorhythmic awareness of the environment becomes the basis of its awareness and behavior both diurnally and annually, or 24/7/52.

If an organism becomes aware of the opportunities presented by daytime or nighttime activity, then the Sun coming up or the Sun going down gives the organism a choice of diurnal or nocturnal intelligence. More complex are the opportunities presented by a high tide or a low tide, which is a cycle independent of day and night; and tidal awareness for coastal organisms leads to opportunistic tidal behavior, and therefore tidal intelligence. It is through their tidal intelligence that sea creatures learned how to expand their domain as land creatures with diurnal intelligence.

When a creature's conscious awareness becomes locked into a **gravitational regulator** such as moonrise and moonset, or a **light regulator** such as sunrise and sunset, those cyclically regulated responses evolve as compartmentalized perspectives of the organism's environmental awareness. Could basic gravitational feeling-responses indeed have evolved into our capacity for **subjective** feelings? And could basic light-activated behavior indeed have evolved as our capacity for **objective** motivation? Could full moons have attracted gatherings that evolved into our capacity for **inter-subjective** communion? Could the four seasons have become the basis of **inter-objective** organization that got the crops sown and reaped and the hunting trip planned?

It is self-evident how the time of day, the time of moon and the time of year affect our survival and social activities, but not so obvious is how these biorhythm-based activities have evolved our awareness into such a complexity that we no longer make the connection between biorhythms and awareness. Throughout history human cultures preeminently honored and celebrated the biorhythmic cycles that gave them life through the moons and seasons. So it is time to consider a few home truths from our ivory tower.

Biorhythms respond to the fluctuations of two main fields of Energy: **Gravitation**, which mainly involves the Moon's orbit around the Earth, and **Electromagnetism**, which mainly involves the Earth's exposure to solar radiation in its orbit around the Sun.

The main resulting gravitational biorhythms are: the Lunar Day of 25 hours from moonrise to moonrise, or one Proximate Tide Cycle; the Lunar Week of seven proximate tide cycles; the Lunar Month of 27 proximate tide cycles, which exactly equals one Lunar Perigee Orbit of 28 days; and the Lunar Year of 13 Perigee Orbits, which equals a Solar Year of one Earth orbit. A Perigee Orbit results from the Lunar orbit being egg-shaped, where the Moon at Perigee is at its closest pass to Earth, and 14 days later it is at its furthest pass in Apogee. This gravitational fluctuation is a key regulator in lunar biorhythms.

And the main electromagnetic biorhythms are: the Solar Day of 24 hours from sunrise to sunrise; the Solar Week of seven axial rotations of the Earth; a Season of 13 Solar Weeks from a Solstice to an Equinox, or Equinox to a Solstice; and a Solar Year from one Winter Solstice to the next.

So a Lunar Year is **7** proximate tides x **4** weeks Perigee Month x **13** Perigee Months = 364 days.

And a Solar Year is **7** axial rotations x **13** weeks Season x **4** Seasons = 364 days.

364 + 1 "Day Out Of Time", as the day of Winter Solstice, is the fabled Soli-Lunar Year of many ancient cultural traditions that honor the beauty of the balance between the Solar and Lunar cycles. The beauty of this balance is also exemplified by the fact that the Luminaries themselves, the Sun and Moon, appear exactly the same size from Earth. To see them in perfect eclipse as mere random happenstance is a denial of the Kosmic Poetry, considering the all-impossible odds that their relative sizes, distances and orbits bring them into perfect balance from our perspective on Earth.

Now we take a closer look at the Eight Fundamental Biorhythms to see if they contain any possible causal links to our Eight Fundamental Perspectives. Self-evident is that **small cycles** are oriented towards **individual** experience, while **large cycles** embrace a more **collective** experience. **Gravitational cycles** induce a more **interior** experience, while **electromagnetic cycles** induce a more **exterior** experience. Already we have the makings of Wilber's Integral model.

1. The 25 hour Lunar Day. This lunar gravitational cycle causes the **Tidal Biorhythm**, which regulates an organism's activities throughout the tidal cycle **from moonrise** (proximal low tide) **to moonrise** (proximal low tide). The moon rises approximately one hour later every day. From an evolutionary point of view this is a very archaic biorhythm, which enabled the emergence of sea creatures on to land, and is therefore opportunistically motivated. Low tide and high tide afforded an organism new survival and evolutionary opportunities. The tide cycle shifts relative to the day cycle, randomly exposing the organism to the day feeding predators. Survival was won with intelligence.

The experiential learning by these opportunities became the core of survival intelligence, and the core of all subsequent types of intelligence as consciousness structures. When our individual survival instincts expand to include others, then learning to emote with their needs becomes the core of our emotional intelligence. When we rationalize our experience, then learning to calculate our opportunities becomes the core of our rational intelligence. We learn to identify with all these experiential Cognitive Structures as our **Cognitive "I"** on the Cube (Octant 2).

2. The 7 Day Lunar Week. One week of tides takes us from a low tide at a given time of day (e.g. Noon) to a high tide. This is the basis of **Tidal Septal Biorhythm**, which tracks the Tidal transition through the Diurnal Biorhythm. Vulnerable nocturnal tidal zone feeders use this to lock into a transitional nocturnal pattern.

Feeling the weekly transit through our inner tides gives us a different feeling about each day, even if our diurnal routine remains unchanged. Nobody knows how far back in our cultural history the seven days of this cycle were given their names Monday through Sunday, but the Seven Calendar Days cycle has remained unbroken ever since, surviving cultural collapses and calendar reforms like some heart beat of humanity. Each day we identify with something different, according to the day, such as a Day of Rest, or Market Day (*Mercredi* – French). The individual identity assumed by each of the Seven Calendar Days hints of a deep and undying individual identification rooted in the core of our being. It is here where we learn to subjectively identify with our **Proximal "I"** on the Cube (Octant 1).

3. The Four Week Lunar Month. The Moon has an egg-shaped or elliptic orbit around the Earth, so that every 28 days it takes a "close pass", which is called Perigee. This monthly gravitational tug or pulse causes the **Lunar Perigee Biorhythm**, an ancient deep-sea and deep psyche trigger causing the monthly Peak Tide. Women are especially affected by this cycle, which regulates ovulation and menstruation. The impact on men seems to be less evident. In cultures worldwide it is traditional for women in collective menstruation to come together in mutual care and concern and deal with sensitive and intimate internal issues. The Lunar Month of Four Lunar Weeks is the collective extension of the quest for our **Cultural Identity "We"** on the Cube (Octant 3).

4. The Thirteen Month Lunar Year. An entire year of Lunar Perigee orbits synchronizes with one Earth orbit on, or immediately after, Winter Solstice. The **Lunar Year Biorhythm** is the first to trigger new cycles of growth in Winter, when the Sun is at its weakest and the Moon reaches its annual zenith or highest elevation in the sky. A Lunar Year of Perigee gravitational pulses synchronizes collective gravitation cycles such as herding instincts, migrations, tribal gatherings and community rituals, which reinforce the collective bonding of scattered communities as the **Cultural Community "We"** on the Cube (Octant 4).

5. The 24 Hour Solar Day. Here we switch from lunar gravitation to the effects of solar electromagnetism on the Earth. One axial rotation of the Earth, from sunrise to sunrise, causes the **Circadian or Diurnal Biorhythm**, which regulates an organism's activities through a 24-hour Day/Night cycle. Because of the Earth's axial tilt, day length varies according to the time of year, which serves as a climate generator. Day length and seasonal climate are therefore modulators of the diurnal biorhythm. An organism's cycle of daily activity is an objective, behavioral routine with which we identify as "my life". This is our **Behavioral Persona "My"** on the Cube (Octant 6).

6. The Seven Day Solar Week. Like the Moon, the Sun also has a 28-day axial rotation as seen from Earth, which produces the **Septal Diurnal biorhythm**. Solar radiation through one solar axial rotation passes through four phases of particle emission, alternating between a week of mostly positive-charged positrons and a week of negative-charged electrons. This cycle radically affects the Earth's magnetosphere, and in turn the cycles of vegetative growth. The Septal Diurnal biorhythm is a pituitary trigger for an intuitive identification with environmental changes. It is here where we learn to identify with our self-referential **Distal Self-image "Me"** on the Cube (Octant 5).

7. The 13 Week Solar Season. Again, because of its axial tilt, the Earth's orbital progress through any Season from Equinox to Solstice or Solstice to Equinox produces the **Seasonal Biorhythm**. The effects of this larger biorhythm are collective, embracing populations. Seasonal changes translate directly into social changes in behavior, such as migration, feeding, mating and hibernation. These collective objectives inspired by a change of Season come with a collective identity to carry them out. Coming together with a common objective, such as harvesting a crop before the first frost, galvanizes the **Social Identity "Us"** on the Cube (Octant 7).

8. The Four Season Solar Year. Earth's orbit of the Sun, returning through Four Seasons to Winter Solstice, causes the **Solar Annual Biorhythm**. No such biorhythm results from the Calendar Year – the Sidereal Year, which is based on Earth's orbital return to a fixed star. Winter Solstice, when the nights are longest and the Sun at its lowest position, re-synchronizes all solar biorhythms.

The Solstice Year is twenty minutes shorter than the Calendar Year – the Calendar Year being set by the Sun's orbital return through the constellations back to a fixed star. Because of the Solstice/Calendar Year discrepancy, Winter Solstice over the years comes earlier and earlier than the Calendar New Year's Day – at the rate of one whole day every 72 years. Because it is more natural that New Year's Day is celebrated on "the Day Out of Time" at Winter Solstice, every few hundred years there is a "Calendar Reform" when the discrepancy becomes socially and naturally intolerable, and they are resynchronized. A year of seasonal changes, returning to Winter Solstice, takes collective objectives from seed to fruition, literally and metaphorically. This is the **Social Order "Our"** on the Cube (Octant 8).

The numbers given to the above Soli-Lunar cycles are also those of the Eight Fundamental Perspectives, so they indeed do seem to have their roots in our Eight Fundamental Biorhythms. But there is one more Biorhythm that concerns the inter-relationship of the Sun, Moon and Earth and serves to integrate our Solar Perspectives with our Lunar Perspectives.

9. The Lunar Synodial Cycle of 29.5 days. This New and Full Moon cycle, or Synodial Month, integrates both electromagnetic and gravitational cycles through the alignment of the Sun, Moon and Earth. As the **Lunar Synodial Biorhythm**, the New/Full Moon Cycle is a larger cycle that serves the collective integration of socio-cultural activity. Twelve New/Full Moon pairs complete the **Eclipse Year** of 348 days, with the Eclipse pairs occurring in the first and seventh Synodial Months. Mating, hunting, planting, reaping and all festive communal activity have forever been celebrated under the various full moons.

It would therefore appear that the Eight Fundamental Perspectives, via Soli-Lunar Cycles, conform to a fundamental cosmological template by which life on this planet has unfolded into complex sentient awareness. Primarily, the Eight Fundamental Perspectives form an archetypal map that gives an organism a dependable basis for orientation and navigation in a world of changes that challenge survival with awareness. This being the case, one would expect to find evidence of the Eight Fundamental Perspectives throughout our cultural history. This is indeed so, starting with the very ancient Creation story of most Native Americans and Meso-Americans. Their cosmological map is encoded by the Six Directions, shown in Figure 14.

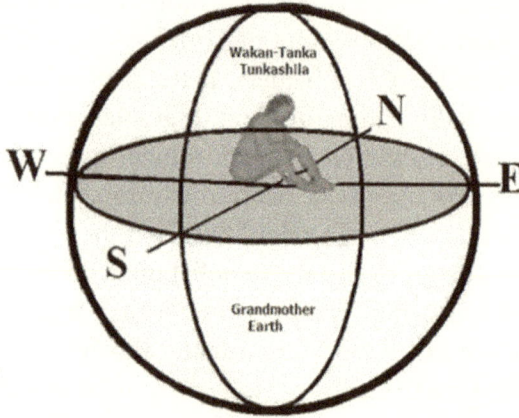

Figure 14. The Six Directions Cosmos of the Native Americans

With **Father** Sky and **Mother** Earth as the Axis, **East** represents the **Individual Path** of Vision Quest; **South** is the **Outgoing Path** of Life; **West** is the **Communal Path** of Ancestors; **North** is the **In-going Path** of Spirit. Yes, the Six Faces of Spirit! In addition, each Direction has its own sacred Mountain. Living in each of the Four Mountains are the Four Talking Gods, who bestow directional Wisdom (Consciousness). "Sacred Mountain" is a metaphor for Subtle Realm, so the Talking Gods are the subtle embodiments of the Four Spirit Realms. Once more we have the Eight Fundamental Perspectives born of the Six Directions.

The story goes on to say that the ancestors first emerged into this present world era from five previous "World Eras" on lower levels, through an opening in the center of the continent. As in previous eras, they were told to go on a clockwise migration of the land to visit each of the Talking Gods and obtain the Four Wisdoms for living in this present world. So this cosmology, by including previous world levels or world-views, is also fully integral.

It is interesting to note that each World Era lasted 5200 years according to the Mayans, and that 5 Eras are 26,000 years, which is one precessional cycle, a Platonic Great Year, or wobble of the Earth on its axis. That is one heck of a Cultural Cycle, the completion of which on Winter Solstice 2012 indeed did get the attention of a global humanity.

We get an incredible insight of the past Great Year as a Cultural Cycle of Four Great Seasons, lasting 6,500 years each. It began as an "Eden" with the Magdalena and Lasceaux cave paintings some 24,000 BCE - art that even to modern standards are works of genius. And the last Great Season, (ironically "Fall") starting with the Biblical "fall" of Eden around 4500 BCE, embraces all the "Great Civilizations" leading to the present.

Another equally ancient cosmology is the Chinese *I Ching*. The primal polarity, through recombination, conceived the Four Bigrams of primordial Space-time, shown as a cubic Tree of Life in Figure 7.

The next stage, through further recombination, resulted in the Eight Trigrams. They were "seen" on the back of a turtle's eight plates by Fu Hsi, an Enlightenment teacher some 5000 years ago. The eight triplet codons of the AQAL Cube shown in Figure 5 are identical to the Eight Trigrams of the *I Ching*, as symbols of the Eight Directions of Kosmic unfolding, or the Eight Fundamental Perspectives shown in Figure 15.

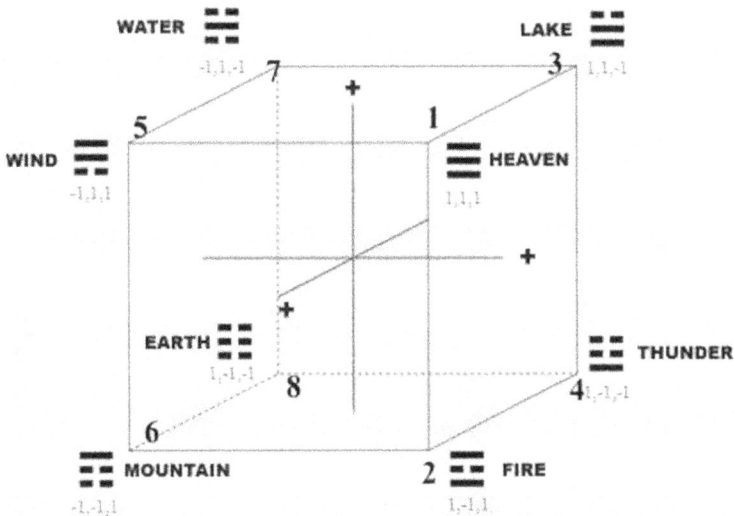

Figure 15. The Eight Trigrams as the Eight Fundamental Perspectives

In the anonymous ancient Taoist Enlightenment treatise *The Secret Of The Golden Flower*, the eight stages of the breath cycle ("Movement of Breath") follows this same sequence of trigram po-larities, moving clockwise, shown in Figure 16.

Wheel of Earlier Heaven

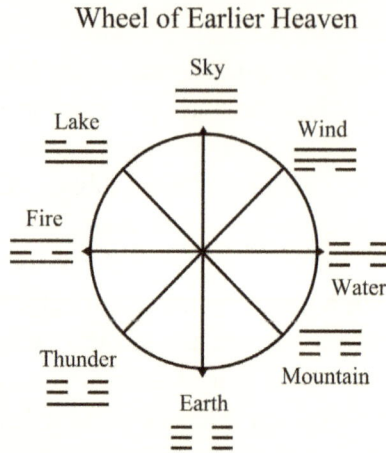

Figure 16. Eight Stages of the Breath Cycle as Trigrams

Note that once again "breath" as *spira* is related to "Consciousness" as *Spiritus,* the message being that consciousness of breath leads to Consciousness of Spirit. Moving clockwise, whether through a breath, a day or a year cycle, the in-breath begins below in Earth/Mid-Night/ Winter; mid-in-breath in Fire/Dawn/Spring; full in-breath in Sky/ Noon/Summer; and mid-out-breath in Water/Evening/Fall.

It is becoming very apparent why most ancient cosmological models also served as Enlightenment models: precisely because the cosmic unfolding of Energy is accompanied by the unfolding of Consciousness. By their very nature, Enlightenment cosmologies never contradict each other; rather they fill in each others' gaps in a bigger picture. For example, the Enlightenment teacher Fu Hsi's Trigram Wheel polarities will be seen to mesh perfectly with the Buddha's Truth Wheel (*Dharmachakra*), which we deal with next.

So it was no coincidence when, 2500 years after Fu Hsi, Gautama Buddha presented a similar cosmological model. Gautama Buddha's Eightfold Path (*Dharmachakra*) is a completely Integral enlightenment model when combined with his Four Noble Truths. The *Dharmachakra*, or Wheel of Truth, describes the Eight Fundamental Perspectives as Enlightenment pre-requisites. They divide the 24 hours into 8 Watches of 3 hours each, so that a three-hour practice of each perspective takes care of each and every day.

The Eight Fundamental Perspectives in Figure 17 are polarity pairs numbered as the eight watches:

1. Understanding – Midnight.
2. Awareness / Intention – 3am.
3. Speech – 6am.
4. Action – 9am.
5. Livelihood – Noon.
6. Effort – 3pm.
7. Thought / Mindfulness – 6pm.
8. Concentration / Absorption – 9pm.

Below the horizon 6pm – 6am are the **Interior Watches**; Midnight – Noon are the **Individual Watches**. Above the horizon 6am – 6pm are the **Exterior Watches**; and Noon – Mid-night are the **Collective Watches**.

Once again we have the Integral map of Eight Fundamental Perspectives. Moving clockwise, the 24-hour cycle starts at Midnight with "Right Understanding", corresponding with "Earth" on the Trigram Wheel.

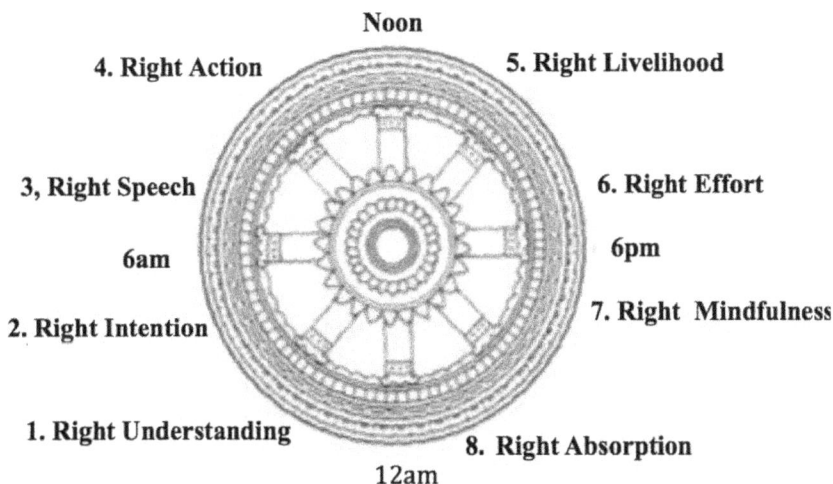

Noon

4. Right Action   5. Right Livelihood

3, Right Speech   6. Right Effort

6am   6pm

2. Right Intention   7. Right Mindfulness

1. Right Understanding   8. Right Absorption

12am

Figure 17. The Eightfold Path

The Four Noble Truths –Suffering, Awareness of Suffering, Awareness of an End to Suffering, and the End of Suffering in the Right Practice of the Eightfold Paths/Perspectives – are four Levels of *Dharmachakra* awareness from ignorance to Buddhahood. At the base of the Buddhist Tree of Life, the *Stupa*, is a Cube representing this Earth plane of existence. Some have inscribed on the eight corners the Eightfold Path attributes.

The Cube has featured many times in the past as a cosmological archetype, such as in the cubic format of the Jewish Tree of Life, or *Kabbalah,* with its Eight (plus One central) *Sephiroth* perspectives. *Kabbalah* is a Semitic derivative of the Arabic *Qaaba* meaning "Cube" and *Al Lah* meaning "God". *Qaaba Al Lah* (Kabbalah) means "Cube of God" as found in the central square at Mecca. The Tree of the Kabbalah is at the heart of Jewish cosmology, and it would take up a book in itself. Suffice it to say here that the Nine Spheres are as profound a model as the *Dharmachakra* and the Trigrams.

It is cross-culturally, however, in the roots of world languages that we find the most ancient description of the Eight Fundamental Perspectives. We know them as the Personal Pronouns. The personal

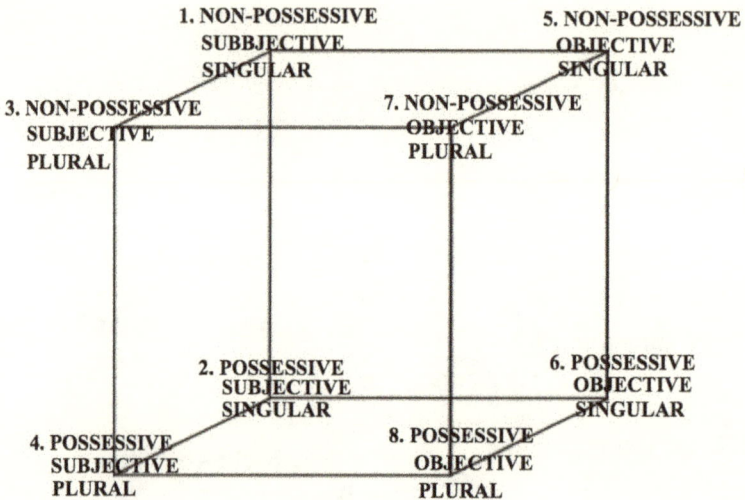

Fig. 18. The Personal Pronouns Cube.

pronouns are the foundation of any language: "Me Tarzan, you Jane". Wilber allocates the AQAL Square with a personal pronoun perspective for each of the Four Quadrants: First Person "I" and "We" to the Upper and Lower Left, and Third Person "It" and "Its" to the Upper and Lower Right. However, languages as a whole differentiate eight personal pronouns **per Person** in exactly the same way as the Eight Fundamental Perspectives of Figure 6, as shown in Figure 18.

Like the Six Faces of Spirit, the Personal Pronouns Cube has six polarities: a Singular, a Plural, a Subjective, an Objective, an intangible Non-Possessive above and a tangible Possessive below. Through recombination this results in $2 \times 2 \times 2 =$ Eight Fundamental Perspectives. Applying the above Figure 18. format to the First Person pronouns gives the AQAL Cube of Eight Fundamental First Person Perspectives, shown in Figure 19.

The first thing that is apparent is how the Non-Possessive Quadrants 1,3,5 and 7 are intangible First Person identities, and how the Possessive Quadrants 2,4,6 and 8 are tangible First Person attributes

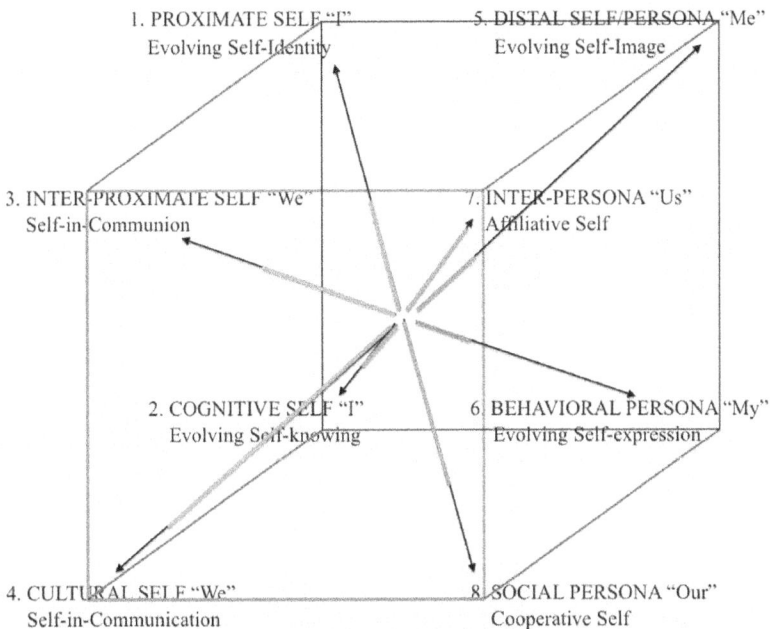

Figure 19. The First Person AQAL Cube

of those identities. The second thing we notice about the First Person Cube is that there is no differentiation in English between the two "I's" and "We's" as First Person pronouns in the Subjective Octants 1,2,3 and 4. Language is a two-way street: On the one hand it identifies pre-existing perspectives as a common experience, which then become "cultural givens"; but on the other hand, in naming them, some perspectives can be culturally biased at the expense of others. Cultures that are objective diminish the subjective; cultures that are collective diminish the individual; cultures that are materialistic diminish the non-material – by not differentiating them. In Russian there is a differentiation between an "inner We" and an "outer collective We" as in "We the people". In Yiddish there is a differentiation between "I" as a spiritual identity and the "I" of everyday life.

It is the very differentiation between the Intangible and the Tangible First Person pronouns that is our main clue to humanity's ancient cultural awareness of the two Domains of self-awareness – the intangible Subtle Consciousness and the tangible Concrete Mind. We now look at these.

Chapter Six

DIFFERENTIATING CONSCIOUSNESS AND MIND

I N BOTH WESTERN science and Integral Theory the terms "consciousness" and "mind" are used synonymously, and in a Concrete context. In this chapter we play hardball with the Integral model and come to grips with the deficiencies of Wilber's AQAL Square in using consciousness and mind synonymously. The immediate effect of their differentiation as the First Person AQAL Cube is a vastly improved psychosocial, psychological and psychotherapeutic model, which we also discuss.

Wilber came very close to differentiating consciousness and mind when he explained the "I/We" anomaly as an Inside "I" and an Outside "I"; an Inside "We" and an Outside "We". From *Integral Spirituality* (2006) [Octant designations in brackets are the author's]:

*– for example, the experience of an "I" in the UL Quadrant. That "I" can be looked at from the **inside** or the **outside**. I can experience my own "I" from the inside [Octant 1], in this moment, as the felt experience of being a subject of my present experience, a 1st person having a 1st person experience. If I do so, the results include such things as introspection, meditation, phenomenology, contemplation, and so on (all simply summarized as phenomenology... But I can also approach this "I" from the outside [Octant 2], in the stance of an objective or*

"scientific" observer. I can so in my own awareness (when I try to be "objective" about myself, or try to "see myself as others see me")... Likewise, I can approach the study of a "we" from its inside or its outside. From the inside [Octant 3], this includes the attempts that you and I make to understand each other right now. How is it that you and I can reach a mutual understanding about anything, including when we simply talk to each other? How do your "I" and my "I" come together in something you and I both call "we" (as in, "Do you and I – do we – understand each other?"). The art and science of we-interpretation is typically called hermeneutics.

But I can also attempt to study this "we" from the outside [Octant 4], perhaps as a cultural anthropologist, or an ethnomethodologist, or a Foucauldian archaeologist...And so on around the quadrants. Thus, 8 basic perspectives and 8 basic methodologies.

In other words, Wilber completely endorses the Left Octants (1,2,3 and 4) of the First Person AQAL Cube, as the *Proximate Self* "I", *Cognitive Self* "I", *Inter-Proximate Self* "We" and *Cultural Self* "We", as shown in Figure 19, but he does not extend this argument to the First Person Right Hand Quadrants (5, 6, 7 and 8). He does, however, begin to address the objective-self issue:

*If you get a sense of yourself right now – simply notice what it is that you call "you" – you might notice at least two parts to this self: one, there is some sort of **observing self** (an inner subject or watcher); and two, there is some sort of **observed self** (some objective things that you can see or know about yourself... The first is experienced as an "I", the second as a "me"... I call the first the proximate self (since it is closer to "you"), and the second the distal self (since it is objective and "farther away").*

The Proximate and Distal Selves are Octant 1 and Octant 5 differentiations on the First Person AQAL Cube. Octant 5 is the *Distal Self* "Me", or the way I formulate my Proximate Self as a *Persona* in its true etymological sense, as my mask, as how "I" want others to identify with "Me". This All Level "Me" is Wilber's "inside" observed self. (Note: This description of the Distal Self as Persona is *not the persona* of fulcrum 4 in Integral Theory.) And the corresponding behavior of this Persona as "My" *Personality* is Wilber's "outside", where Octant 6 pertains to "My" personality through "My" behavior. The Enneagram personality types, as elucidated by Don Riso (1987), makes the Persona/Personality differentiation very clearly. Equally, our *Social Persona* or our identification with "Us" "inside", and our *Social Personality* behavior in "Our" tribe "outside", follow the same First Person differentiations.

These eight important First Person Self-differentiations have not yet been made in Integral Psychology, even though they are experientially self-evident to the point where Wilber himself has discussed seven, including "Mine" and "Us". Nevertheless our Eight Fundamental Perspectives *in First Person* remain a blind spot in Integral Theory.

Wilber's added "Inside-Outside" polarity doubled his Four Fundamental Perspectives to Eight Third Person "Zones" and Eight "Methodologies". At this point it becomes clear that languages do provide for Eight Fundamental Perspectives as Eight Personal Pronouns *per Person*, as shown in Figures 20a, 20b and 20c.

(a) First Person Cube

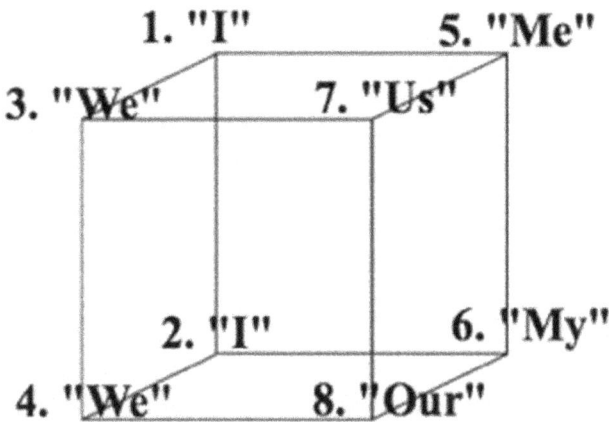

1. "I"   5. "Me"
3. "We"   7. "Us"
2. "I"   6. "My"
4. "We"   8. "Our"

(b) Second Person Cube

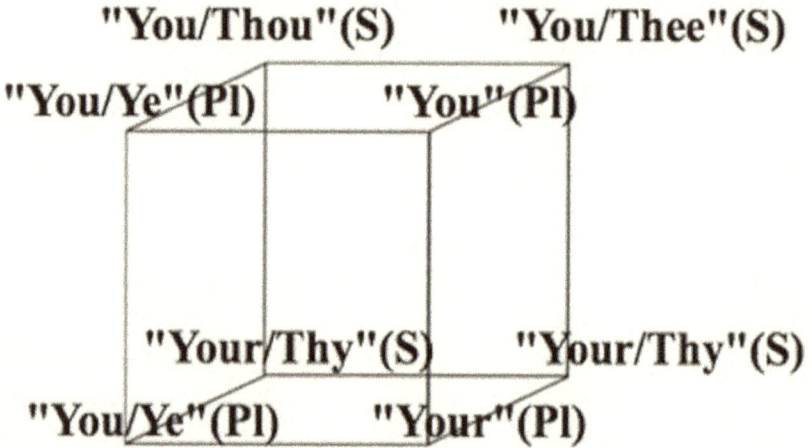

"You/Thou"(S)   "You/Thee"(S)

"You/Ye"(Pl)   "You"(Pl)

"Your/Thy"(S)   "Your/Thy"(S)

"You/Ye"(Pl)   "Your"(Pl)

(c) Thirs Person Cube

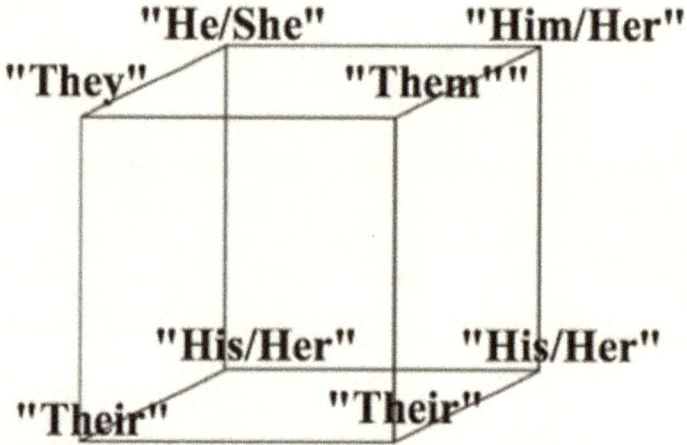

"He/She"   "Him/Her"

"They"   "Them"""

"His/Her"   "His/Her"

"Their"   "Their"

Figure 20. First, Second and Third Person Personal Pronoun Cubes

The Third Person Pronouns Cube above goes to the Third Person (Impersonal) Cube, as Wilber's Eight Fundamental Perspectives of Integral Methodological Pluralism, shown in Figure **21**.

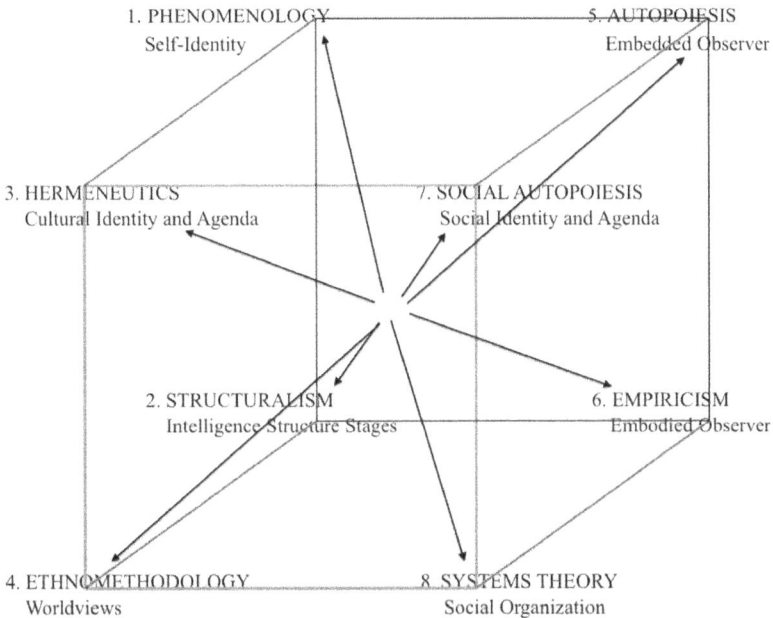

Figure 21. Third Person (Impersonal) AQAL Cube

However, Wilber *did not define the injunction* that would explain his added "Inside-Outside" polarity, to form the above Eight Fundamental Perspectives. As a result, Integral Theory has *not been able to explain* the self-evident fact that we *can* take "Inside" (Internal, Non-Possessive) and "Outside" (External, Possessive) views, and that our capacity to do so is in some way a consciousness capacity. I propose that the AQAL Cube's Subtle and Concrete Quadrants (Octants), as Consciousness and Mind, are *synonymous with*, and *numbered as*, Wilber's Eight "Inside" and "Outside" Perspectives.

In other words, the key to differentiating Consciousness from Mind is in how our *Consciousness-as-experiencer* does indeed view through our *Mind-as-experience*. It is interesting to note that while Wilber does not differentiate his "Inside" and "Outside" perspectives as Subtle Consciousness and Concrete Mind, in his (2004) *Kosmos Trilogy* (Excerpt D, p. 160) he actually does follow Aurobindo in correlating the experiential levels of *Mind* with levels of *Cognitive awareness* (aka *Access awareness*):

Aurobindo's use of 'Supermind' was quite specific; in a sense, it is the first form of manifestation in a transformed bodymind. Still, the word 'Supermind' has escaped into popular parlance and taken on a life of its own; I use it as a generalized term for the highest recognizable wave of cognitive development, even if that wave has only appeared in a few and is thus not yet any sort of universal structure or kosmic habit.

This is exactly how the First Person AQAL Cube maps the Cognitive Self (Octant 2), as Mind through the Levels from proto-mind to Super-Mind.

Also of interest is how the various Lines in Integral Theory's Self System (in the AQAL Square Upper Left) have an eerie correspondence with the Eight First Person Perspectives. Naturally, this needs to be played out in Integral Research, but I propose that the correspondence self-evidently corroborates the First Person AQAL Cube (Figure 19).

This opens a giant can of worms for Integral Theory, which others have already opened. Wendelin Kupers (2009) in his "*The Status and Relevance of Phenomenology for Integral Research*" begins by saying:

"*The goal of this undertaking is to show that phenomenology – particularly in its more advanced forms – is more and different than something to put merely into "upper left" quadrant or to understand only as a "Zone 1" affair suggested in the conventional integral model...*" He then continues,

"*Consciousness is always what is seen and felt (psychic-intentional) and embodied and enacted (behavioral) within a socio-cultural (the other) and systemic nexus. If we see that the phenomenological space or medium of consciousness is inherently related to the entire AQAL space, then we need considering further advanced phenomenological approaches to consciousness and mind (e.g., Gallagher, 2007; Gallagher & Zahavi, 2005, 2008) and with this, more inter-subjective and inter-relational perspectives...*" [author's bold].

The First Person AQAL Cube completely opens up Phenomenology to eight *experiential* perspectives we have of ourselves and of this world; and it is hoped that phenomenological and transpersonal research, especially with inter-subjective and inter-personal perspectives, can start modeling these via the Personal Perspectives catalogued in the *Appendix*.

In the *Appendix* are listed in detail the Eight First Person, the Eight Second Person and Eight Third Person Perspectives, for those who wish to pursue this further. Needless to say there is a tremendous potential here for an expanded First and Second Person therapeutic model, when we consider that most of our life is spent in First-to-Second Person relationships and that to be able to model inter-relationships in the expanded detail of First and Second Person Cubes would vastly contribute to our understanding of Octant-specific dysfunctionality.

In the *Appendix* we also pursue this line of inquiry into the need for such a detailed Persons – Perspectives model for delicate inter-subjective and inter-personal situations, not only for therapy but also for justice, leadership, political and diplomatic relations. Justice, for example, is an "I / You" and "We / You" dynamic, as well as "I / Them" and "We / Them". For justice to be served, all the information pertaining to "I", "We", "You" and "Them" needs to be differentiated for proper consideration, including the Levels from which that information is coming. All this is then weighed against the FACTS, which are located on the Third Impersonal Cube of This and That It and These and Those Its. This is the most exacting enactment of "Wilber's "Perspectives taking Perspectives", which in turn are the precursors of the resulting Perceptions. All of this nuance cannot be meaningfully integrated without expanding the Personal Pronoun Perspectives to their full potential.

An example of such "full potential" concerns the injustice of political and economic disenfranchisement for most of the people on this planet – an "Us and Them" dynamic. The failure of systems to help the poor while empowering the wealthy has led to most of the world-wide economic and ecologic devastation. On all four AQAL Cubes, systems failure as matters of justice and injustice, or equilibrium and disequilibrium, are mapped by Octants 7 and 8 through the Three Persons.

If Integral Theory and Practice is to play a meaningful role here, the author strongly suggests that the expanded AQAL Cubes model be used to map the areas of political and economic dysfunctionality, from which warfare is the usual outcome. As of this writing, an estimated 68 million people have been displaced from their homes and homelands through the ravaging triangulation of greed, famine and war.

The rest of this chapter is dedicated to demonstrating potential Integral therapeutic applications of the First Person AQAL Cube. From the outset we need to remember that our Second and Third Person Perspectives are our own objects viewed by our own First Person subjects. There is nothing "out there" that is not already "in here", and "perspectives taking perspectives" means we are always taking binary perspectives, as our subject taking an object.

The whole point of an Integral model is to use it as a tool to further the evolution of our self, our culture and others. With the AQAL Cube there is huge potential for an expanded psychoanalytical map, with associated therapies. Using the AQAL Cube's 24 Perspectives through the first Three Persons gives us a greatly expanded model to chart our evolution through the Quadrants in a balanced way towards Causal existence and awareness. It is therefore crucial for our individual development, in the author's opinion, that we have a First Person Eight Perspectives model to serve as an Integral Psychograph.

Here is a simple demonstration of the *First Person AQAL Cube as an Integral Psychograph*, to evaluate our client "Bob" with a questionnaire and find his altitude in each of his Eight First Person Perspectives. The AQAL Cube Psychograph, Figure 22, shows how the altitude of each Perspective can be represented as a color on the Wilber-Newtonian Spectrum.

Evaluating a Client "Bob" Through Eight First Person Perspectives:

1. **Proximate Self "I",** (Inside, Subjective, Singular). Bob's altitude here is his benchmark for self-referencing throughout the Octants. From this altitude, Bob as the Witness-experiencer colors the nature of all his experience. Questioning about his inmost sense of self, of who he feels he really is, reveals his level of self-referencing.

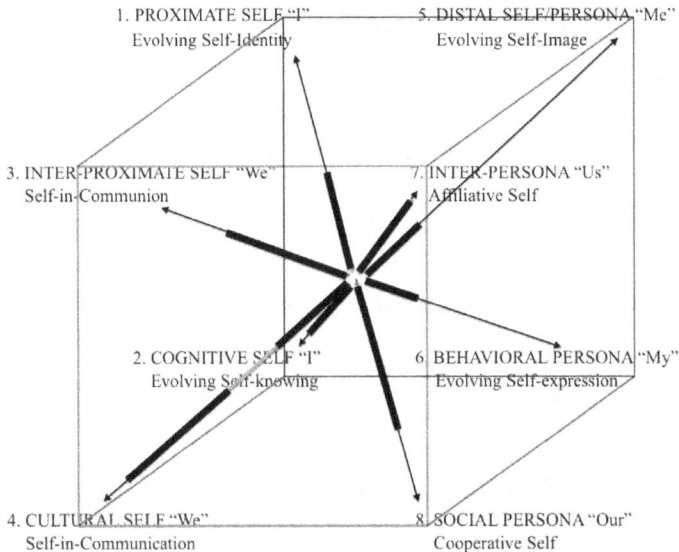

Figure 22. The AQAL Cube Psychograph

2. **Cognitive Self "I"**, (Outside, Subjective, Singular). Bob's altitude here colors the nature of his experience as his thoughts and feelings, rationale and vision. Questioning these, as all the Lines of Intelligence, reveals his levels of cognition.

3. **Inter-Proximate Self "We"**, (Inside, Subjective, Plural). Here is Bob's shared identity, how he reveals his sense of self to someone else, and his capacity to understand where someone else is coming from. Questioning these reveals his level of inter-proximate awareness.

4. **Inter-Cognitive Self "We"**, (Outside, Subjective, Plural). Here Bob shares his thoughts, feelings and worldviews, according to his cognitive capacity. Questioning these reveals his levels of inter-cognitive awareness.

5. **Distal Self "Me"**, (Inside, Objective, Singular). This is Bob's self-image, how he identifies himself as a person. This is therefore his All-Level Persona, his mask through which he can formulate the uniqueness of his "intentional persona" (Enneagram). Questioning about his self-image and its intentions reveals his level of Persona.

6. **Behavioral Personality "My"**, (Outside, Objective, Singular). Bob expresses his Distal Self through his Behavioral Personality.

Again, this is uniquely his, and by which others know Bob as Bob. Here Bob is the most empirically revealing as to the level he is coming from.

7. **Inter-Distal Self "Us",** (Inside, Objective, Plural). This is Bob's Social Self-image, through which he objectively identifies with other friends, family, colleagues and affiliates. Questioning about these relationships reveals his level of inter-personal or social identity.

8. **Social Personality "Our",** (Outside, Objective, Plural). Here Bob shows his social skills in cooperative behavior and ethical conduct. Questioning about these reveals his level of Social behavior.

The author suggests that an Integral psychotherapist tries evaluating clients through a Self-system psychograph of Eight First Person Perspectives, and differentiates them as a Consciousness-Mind dynamic by which their clients can be navigated through the Levels of each Octant. Transitioning from one Cognitive Level to the next on Octant 2 is called a Fulcrum Shift, where a fulcrum is like a rung on the Cognitive Ladder. So when we talk about the Self-system as navigating through developmental fulcrum Levels, we are dealing on the one hand with identity shifts in Consciousness (Climber) and on the other hand with correlated cognitive fulcrum shifts of Mind (Ladder). Because of this, to integrate eight Self-Octants is a far more complex process than Integral Theory describes.

On the First Person AQAL Cube a fulcrum shift is primarily an "Individual Quadrants" Tetra-Dynamic, a complex integration between all four "Individuals" Octants 1, 2, 5 and 6; where stable Subjective identity shifts (Octants 1 and 2) also need to be accompanied by stable Objective identity shifts (Persona, and Behavioral Personality, Octants 5 and 6), shown in Figure 23

The author proposes that there are *four stages* to completing a fulcrum shift. STAGE 1: when our Proximate Self "I" (Octant 1) transcends to its next Level of identity, it also enables the previous Cognitive Self "I" fulcrum (Octant 2) to shift to its next correlated structural Level of cognition. During this transition the Proximate Self objectifies the previous Cognitive "I". STAGE 2: the Proximate Self shift also causes a new correlated state stage of self-image as the

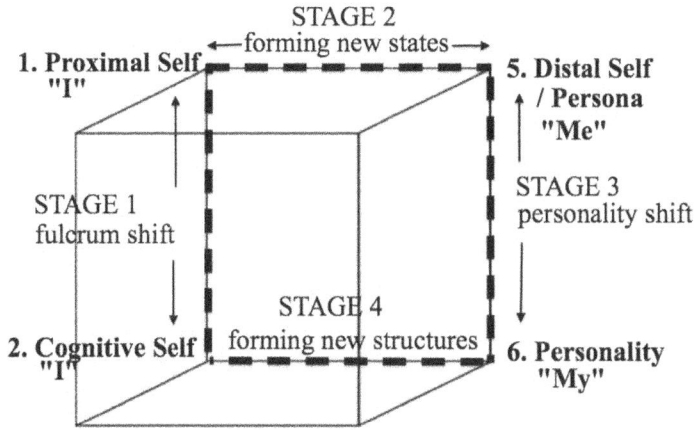

Figure 23. First Person "Individuals" Tetra-Dynamics, Octants 1,2,5,6

Distal Self/Persona "Me" (Octant 5). STAGE 3: those identities then materially consolidate as the next correlated structure stage of "My" Personality (Octant 6.). STAGE 4: the Personality shift then structurally stabilizes with the Cognitive Self.

This is a very complex process where there is many a slip twixt cup and lip. This entire process needs to be re-evaluated using the First Person AQAL Cube Octo-Dynamics, because Integral Theory lacks a First Person AQAL Cube model to map the Octo-Dynamics of psychopathology associated with Fulcrum failures, or to map appropriate psychotherapies.

A very simple example of a psychotherapeutic, First Person "Individuals" Tetra-Dynamic is the breath cycle. In consciously taking and experiencing "My" breath (Octant 6), "I" experience a calming of thoughts (Octant 2), which "I" Witness (Octant 1), as transforming "Me" (Octant 5). This is how the breath cycle can be analyzed as a transformative meditative First Person AQAL Cube practice towards greater self-awareness. In other words, every *self-aware act we undertake* becomes potentially transformative through the above First Person "Individuals" Tetra-Dynamic.

Certain of our Eight Fundamental Perspectives evolve faster than others, partly because of the fixed developmental sequence of unfolding psychological stages; partly because some people are more introverted and others more extroverted; partly because some are more introspective and others more objective; partly because our individual lines of intelligence (instinctual, emotional, rational, moral, spiritual) vary in their levels of development and so on. These are issues we each have to deal with in our own way.

We can process these issues in the same way we just processed our breath cycle. For example, my non-material Self ("I", Octant 1) identifies an innate need or an evolutionary imperative. My material Self ("I", Octant 2) experientially interprets this need as various experiential hungers and psychological urges via its appropriate intelligence structures. And to meet those needs my material organism has to perform some appropriate objective behavior ("My", Octant 6). Depending on whether those needs are correctly identified, interpreted and objectively met, then my objective Persona ("Me", Octant 5) is either satisfied, or it will prompt me to identify a more appropriate intention ("I", Octant 1).

It is clear that there is a great potential for dysfunction and lack of integration of the participating Octants – such as a poor identification of the need (Octant 1), a lack of information and intelligence to correctly interpret the need (Octant 2), poor skills or appropriate behavior to meet the need (Octant 6), or poor objective judgment in satisfying the need (Octant 5).

A simple form of fulcrum dysfunction is when we tend to identify more with one of the Eight First Person Perspectives as our modus operandum, which manifests as a behavioral bias or character trait. For example, we can be predominantly an Introspective (Octant 2), a Personality (Octant 6), a Socialite (Octant 8) or Community Spirit (Octant 4). But we can balance our lopsidedness by integrating the diametrically opposite perspective: the Introspective (Octant 2) finds release in its Social Persona (Octant 7), the superficial personality (Octant 6) finds depth in its Cultural Self (Octant 3), the outgoing Socialite (Octant 8) finds inner peace in its Proximate Self (Octant 1), and the selfless Community Spirit (Octant 4) attends to personal needs in its Persona (Octant 5).

Does the above integration of our Consciousness and Mind feature in our cultural history? Hugely, because our psychological well-being is integral with our social and spiritual well-being. The preachers of world religions have always served to counsel their congregations in the basics of morals, ethics, trauma, relationships and behavioral imbalance. In this regard, the teachings of the four major world religions have done a good job in representing each of the Cube's four diametric axes we have just looked at, as alternative paths of integrating our Consciousness and Mind. In this very over-simplified example, we show how each of the four world religions give emphasis to one or other of these four paths of integration as a result of cultural biases.

To integrate our Proximate Self (Octant 1) with our Social Order and Environment (Octant 8) is the path of integration taught by the Hindu, *Krishna.* He described our being as floating like a lotus in the Sun while being rooted deep in the mud of worldly existence.

Or integrating our Personality (Octant 6) with our Cultural Self (Octant 3) is the path of integration taught by *Buddha.* His doctrine of the Dharma, in which we are individually accountable for the results of our actions, is lived out in our relationship with the Sangha, our spiritual community.

Or integrating our Cognitive Self (Octant 2) with our Social Persona (Octant 7) is the path taught by *Jesus.* He said love your neighbors as your self, where we apply our individual experience in improving social awareness.

Lastly, to integrate our own Persona (Octant 5) with our Community Spirit (Octant 4) is the path of the Culture Hero righting wrongs, establishing rights, the servant-leader in each of us as exemplified by *Mohammed.*

Many more therapeutic techniques can be developed using the tetra-dynamics of each face of the First Person AQAL Cube. We have considered the "Individuals/Singulars" Quadrants, but there are also the "Collectives/Plurals", the "Interiors/Subjectives", the "Exterior/Objectives", the "Insides/Non-Possessives" and the "Outsides/Possessives". In Chapter 11 we make the *correlation of the above six*

Tetra-Dynamics with the six Chakras, where Chakra therapy can be approached using the First Person Perspectives.

The therapeutic value of understanding our Octo-dynamic Self-System is to become more balanced, and in this way facilitate transition through the Fulcrums on *all* Octants. But to go deeper into the Truth of the Self, we need to understand how our perspectives are at the mercy of our perception. We have seen how a bias in perspective perceptually alters our behavior, which then can be balanced through an opposite perspective. But we also operate automatically by personal and socio-cultural "givens" in our Consciousness and Mind perspectives. These "givens" are the perceptual assumptions we make according to the Level of Self we operate from. Then what is the underlying means to enable us to develop beyond our perceptual assumptions, and on through the Levels?

Chapter Seven

CONSCIOUSNESS AND MIND IN PERCEPTION

O UR MAIN PERSONAL "given" in every moment of our life is our perception. How do we come to see our selves, others, and the world, the way we do? Each morning when we wake up and we see everyone and everything differently, what happened?

Perception is how we interpret our awareness, and that interpretation is based on many variables such as which of the **Eight Fundamental Perspectives** we are taking in that moment, which of **the First, Second, Third Persons** etc., and from which **Levels**. And when we then assume that what is being perceived has reality, that assumption in turn gives rise to the illusion of our own identity as the perceiver. "Growing up" is actually the process of becoming lost in our own labyrinth of perceptual relativity and shadow realities.

The mechanics of perception, though seemingly mysterious and complex, operate on a very simple system. To understand this system will help bring all this perceptual relativity to our conscious awareness.

Con-Sciousness means "knowing with" – but to know with what? Early Greek philosophers deduced that perception results from the interaction of three factors: The Knower, the Means of Knowing and the Known. We perceive the world out there as the realm of the Known, which is the realm of Energy, but the problem all the philosophers and empiricists have had throughout the ages is to correctly identify the Knower and the Means of Knowing.

If the Knower is the experiencer, and the Knowing is the experience, then this poses a First Person relativity between two Domains of awareness: between the experiencer as subject and the correlated experience as object. Given that the AQAL Cube's Primary Axis shows how AQAL Subtle existence is embedded in, and embodied by, correlated AQAL Gross (or Concrete) existence, we now need to see how our awareness actually differentiates and correlates the two. More specifically, it is in how our *awareness as Subtle Consciousness* is differentiated from, and correlates with, our *awareness as Concrete Mind*.

The key word here is "*awareness*", in that it is common to both Consciousness and Mind. The word "Awareness" has an Indo-European root. *A Varus* is Latin for "attested truth", which is witnessed truth. So, in common with Subtle Conscious awareness and Concrete Mind awareness is the Witness behind them, meaning that Con-Sciousness is to be witnessing (knowing) through the Subtle lens and Mind is to be witnessing through the Concrete lens. In other words the Knower has two perceptual lenses as Means-of-knowing, which are correlated full-spectrum in both Domains.

To go back to the problem of correctly identifying the Knower and Means-of-knowing, the First Person relativity between the Experiencer and the experience has to do with the relative altitudes between the Witness, Consciousness and Mind. The altitudes here are represented as colors of the Wilber-Newtonian spectrum:

When the *Lower Mind* becomes self-aware in Red, it assumes itself to be the Concrete knower, and the Body its means of knowing. Similarly, when *Consciousness* becomes self-aware in Blue, it assumes itself to be the Subtle knower, and the Mind and Body its Concrete means of knowing. Finally when the *Witness* becomes self-aware in Violet, it no longer assumes, but *is* the Knower with Consciousness as its Subtle experience and Mind and Body as its Concrete experience.

Wilber (2009) again made the Primary Axis injunction by default in differentiating two "Selves": the "Real Self" as climber-experiencer and the "Actual Self" as experiential ladder. We therefore propose that the Real Self is the All-Level Witnessing Self with its experiential Consciousness and the Actual Self is the Cognitive Self with its experiential Mind.

In Wilber's (1996) *Sex, Ecology and Spirituality*, Note 28, p635-6 we read:

> *Plotinus has a remarkable theory of the self, which is still altogether viable. Aside from the notion that we have "two souls" (the timeless witness and the temporal self), the self (or Soul) for Plotinus has two different meanings. One, it is a particular level or dimension of existence – the World Soul (or psychic level). But two, the Soul is what we moderns would call the "self- system", the actual navigator of the great holarchy – not a particular stage but the "traveler" of each stage; not a rung in the ladder but the **climber of the ladder**. As such, **the Soul or self- system can span the entire spectrum of development** [author's bolds] (except the higher limits, where it is transcended or becomes the Absolute)... Development, then, is a case of the Soul growing and expanding, taking more and more of the external world into itself, as Plotinus puts it.*

Wilber has enumerated five developing phases of his work, and in the above "Wilber-4" phase quote he openly implies a full-spectrum Subtle Domain, where his description of an *All-Level Soul-Self* is *exactly* that of Goswami's All-Level *Subtle Consciousness Monad* with its sheathes of awareness shown in Figure 1.

However, for some reason his "Wilber-5" phase goes against this, saying "Soul emerges" in Indigo on the Spectrum. "Wilber-5" is his era of "post-metaphysics", when he cleans house and deposes all the "givens" of metaphysics until they can be proven and re-instated. So an all-level Soul was thrown out with the bathwater. The author recently had an intense email discussion with him about this, the author pointing out that "Soul emerging into our *awareness* in Indigo" is quite valid but *distinct from* "Soul emerging into *existence* from all-the-way-down"; and that they are *not* synonymous. But he remained adamant that Soul coming into existence is completely synonymous with its coming into our awareness as a function of Indigo cognition. Unfortunately, his implication here is that we (and all creatures) are denied a Soul until we achieve Indigo cognition – meaning the entirety of Life save for a few hundred thousand people!

So it now becomes necessary to re-contextualize some established terms in Integral Theory, in order to define the Subtle and Concrete differentiation between Consciousness and Mind as made by the AQAL Cube's Primary Axis injunction. On the one hand we propose to establish the Soul as the Subtle *Consciousness Self* – the self-assuming All-Level knower, experiencer, or First Person *Climber* with a Level-specific witnessing identity. On the other hand we propose to establish its correlated Concrete *Cognitive Self* – the experiential Mind, or the Concrete All-Level means of knowing, or First Person *Ladder* with a Level-specific experiential identity as sensations, feelings and thoughts.

In this light, "Qualia" as experiential phenomena become self-referential perceptions witnessed via a Level-specific Consciousness-Mind dynamic as experiencer and experience, subject and object.

A simple example of qualia as a dynamic between Consciousness and Mind is in that elusive but vital aspect of awareness called "conscience". It is not without significance that the word *"conscience"* in French means "consciousness". Our conscience regarding a situation may literally come though to us as an inner voice, actually advising us, but more usually it is an intuitive feeling that tells us what is right or what is wrong. Where does that voice or feeling come from, and why is it always so right as to be a moral compass? The answers we get come from Level-specific interpretations of Mind, or perception. In the lower spectrum our voice of conscience would be heard as that of our guardian angel, or even of God. Higher up we have gut feelings, sub-conscious intelligence, intuition, being in touch with our feelings, or heart. And even higher, when our Subtle Consciousness has differentiated from our Concrete Mind and we have become Soul-aware, we realize the French had it right all along – it is the voice of our very own Consciousness, as the Distal Self of Octant 5, coming from a place of wisdom our Soul has earned through many lifetimes. This is why our Mind can take no credit for conscience, but only for how it decides to interpret it (Octant 2) and act on it (Octant 6), hopefully with moral and ethical alacrity. However, if the Mind's cognitive awareness is beset with shadow elements, the "voice" of conscience can become distorted as the "voice" of the super-ego, and resultant personality disorders in Octant 6.

At the heart of the matter of perception is how Consciousness and Mind, as Subtle and Concrete awareness respectively, actually make the three axial injunctions. From the onset of its tri-axial unfolding, an embedded and embodied Subtle proto-conscious monad, processing its proto-awareness via its Concrete proto-mind, evolves towards conscious clarity and cognitive complexity respectively.

The work of the cell-biologist Dr. Bruce Lipton (2005) shows that even the simplest eucaryote (a primordial class of unicellular organisms) is a proto-experiencer intending its proto-experience, and consolidating a genome to that effect according to its needs rather than through natural selection. We have come back to intentional evolution, which was first postulated by Lamarck – a contemporary of Darwin.

The primal needs of an organism have not only to do with obtaining the necessities for physical survival, but also with establishing a sentient identity with which to navigate its survival. Survival is favored by greater awareness, and making conscious choices. In the proto-conscious stages an identity simply means the organism's fundamental ability to perceptually differentiate between the inside of its cellular membrane and the outside. The cellular membrane eventually evolves as the epidermis of a multi-cellular organism, which in turn evolves into neural complexity and the brain. This evolving complexity becomes self-awareness and identity issues, which start to make exponential demands on neural processing.

We saw how our Ego-self complex is formed in babyhood by Inertia, Desire and Fear – our reaction formations – which must be overcome in the course of our psychological unfolding. Otherwise, through our Inertia, or Ego-as-doer, we lose our Growth; through our Desires, or Ego-as-enjoyer, we lose our Direction; and through our Fears, or Ego-as-thinker, we lose our Balance. The more embodied and embedded we get, Inertia becomes resistance, Desire becomes attachment, and Fear becomes phobia. So, to overcome these shadow-obstacles of reaction formation we have to evolve new strategies that are contiguous with our fundamental mechanisms of orientation. These strategies invoke the Three Axial Injunctions of the AQAL Cube.

The author proposes that each of the Three Axes arrives at its injunction as a stage of an organism's learning to orientate itself to, and survive in, its environment. The injunction for each axis actuates an unfolding aspect of awareness: The *Id identity* initially engages Subject with Object, or its *Interior* with its *Exterior (First Axis injunction)*, identifying through its survival instincts of hunger, desire, fear etc. The *Ego identity* initially engages its Singular with its Plural, or as an *Individual* in a *Collective (Second Axis injunction)*, identifying through its relational role in the species collective. The *Soul identity* initially engages its Subtle with its Concrete, or its *Inside* with its *Outside (Primary Axis injunction)*, in its capacity to differentiate its Subtle AQAL Consciousness from its correlated Concrete AQAL Mind. Ultimately its core *Witness identity* engages all axes non-differentially in all Domains, Quadrants and Levels through its capacity of non-dual awareness.

Next, the author proposes that the above classic sequence of Self-identification is *the result* of an unfolding Mind/Consciousness as a Primary Axis dynamic: The *Id* is non-self-aware Mind/Consciousness *fused* at a Level of Concrete fascination The *Ego* is Self-aware Mind/Consciousness *fused* at a Level of Concrete identification. The *Soul* is Self-aware Consciousness *differentiated* from Mind at a Level of Subtle identification. Finally, the *Witness* is pure Self-awareness *differentiated* from Consciousness at a Level of Causal identification.

The above stages of differentiation of our Consciousness and Mind cause huge perceptual shifts. The self-aware Mind has power in the Concrete environment. The self-aware Consciousness has power in the Subtle Domain. The self-aware Witness has Causal power. These are mapped in greater dimensionality by Don Beck's

(1996) Spiral Dynamics Integral model, as unfolding through Three Tiers – the mechanics of which *are not* explained by that model but *are* perfectly explained by the AQAL Cube's tri-axial injunctions. Our individual evolution as Knower, Means-of-Knowing and the Known is described below using the *Wilber-Newtonian spectrum* in Figure 24:

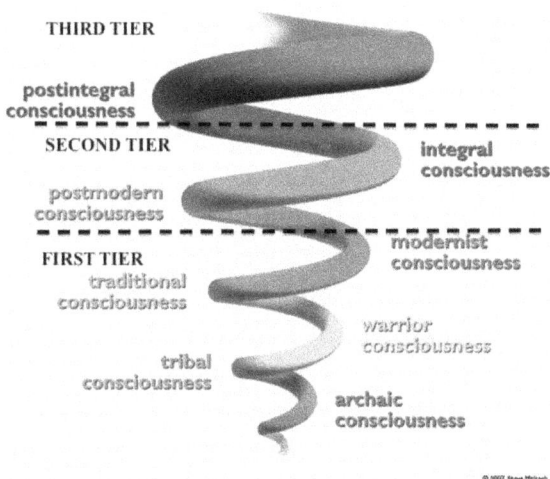

Figure 24. The Developmental Spiral (Wilber-Newtonian Spectrum)

In First Tier, Infra Red through Green, our level of identification is our Concrete existence, where our physically-identified and fused Consciousness, as the *Id (Concrete fascination),* leads to the *Self-aware Ego (autonomous Concrete Self).* This is because our First Tier Consciousness-as-experiencer is so identified with Mind-as-experience as to assume it *is* Mind. It subsequently assumes that Mind is the Knower of the Known out there, and that the Body is its Means of Knowing. This mistaken material Consciousness identity is called Ego.

In Second Tier, Blue through Indigo (Wilber-Newtonian spectrum), our level of identification shifts to our ongoing Subtle existence, and that our subtly-identified Consciousness becomes the *Self-aware Soul (autonomous Subtle Self).* Here, the Soul assumes a spiritual identity, where Consciousness assumes it is the Knower and that the Mind *and* Body are now its mere Means of Knowing. The Ego has been humbled, and this new more subtle (yet still mistaken) Consciousness identity is called Soul. By definition, Soul awareness now becomes truly Psychic, or spiritually aware of its Second Tier existence in the Subtle Domain. This is a big leap of identification, culminating in Indigo with our psychic awareness of Subtle bodies and realms.

This is modeled in the AQAL Cube as the Subtle Quadrants, our Subtle Conscious awareness of which *is* the *Primary Axis injunction*. It is called in Tibetan Buddhist literature "the *turning about in the seat of Consciousness*", meaning our awareness turns from our Concrete to Subtle identity. In his *The Eagle's Gift*, Castaneda calls it "the turning of intent". It is a profound life-changing inner experience. For example, here is where our Higher Mind, the Concrete vehicle of our Soul, comes into play. At this Level the Higher Mind now has the autonomy for non-local, out-of-body psychic experience because it is experientially processing the very fundamental levels of Concrete energy close to the Zero Point Field. In this context of the Primary Axis injunction, Don Beck's claim that not many have yet made Second Tier awareness would seem very much in order.

In Third Tier, Violet through Ultra Violet, our level of identification shifts to our ongoing Causal existence, and that our causally identified Consciousness is the *Self-aware Witness (autonomous Causal Self)*. Here the Soul identity, in becoming aware of Pure Consciousness, shifts to the One Knower; where Soul Consciousness is now yet another mere Means of Knowing along with Mind and Body – a humbling experience indeed. In other words, the Witness, at any Level of the Consciousness Spectrum, is the true Experiencer of all its mistaken identities. Here, in Enlightenment, we are aware of our Subtle and Concrete existence as not-two, as a total integration of our One Being. At this Level, the Witness has the Causal Mind as its vehicle, which is the Universal Mind, or Akasha.

So, in Third Tier the One Knower, as the Supreme Identity (the I Am), ultimately makes Consciousness as transparent as Consciousness had made Mind transparent in Second Tier. From the initially fused proto-conscious/proto-mind monad, Pure Consciousness (as the Supreme Knower) and its Super-Mind (as the Supreme Knowledge) are ultimately not-two. This purity of perception is called Clarity.

The above Three Tiers, as stages of Primary Axis unfolding, can be synonymously described and explained, in First Person terms, by the *Three Levels of Attention*. Our All-Level Consciousness monad identifies with, or attaches to, a specified Level on the Spectrum of Consciousness according to its Level of *Attention* or Self-identification. The At-tention is the Knower "holding on" to that Level. There are three Levels of Attention that exactly correspond to the Three Tiers.

The *First Attention* holds on hard to everyday physical reality. The *Second Attention* lets go of Concrete reality to Subtle reality. The *Third Attention* is the big let-go to Causal reality. From the *Attention*, on whatever Level, Consciousness can operate with *Intention*. The author proposes that In-tention, or the Knower "holding in", is how the Subtle Consciousness initiates its own wave collapse, or more accurately wave extension, from the Subtle to the Concrete frequency band, thereby initiating a Concrete effect through a correlated quantum of Mind. Mind is therefore the *Extension*, the "holding out" of the Subtle Consciousness to transduce an Intention into its coexistent Concrete reality as a "wavicle" of information with Mass; and that Mass then achieves the desired Concrete effect as *En-ergia*, meaning "at work".

The converse is also true: To pass from Mind to Consciousness, such as in meditation, we intend the suspension of Subtle Consciousness transduction into Concrete Mind, resulting in the suspension of Mind as *en-quietus*, which is meditation. The conscious intent of a *First Attention* fused Consciousness/Mind to meditate is to let go of Gross identification, and so dis-identify with the Mind. This is the first step in moving towards a Second Attention perspective. Similarly, the conscious intent of a *Second Attention* Consciousness to meditate is to suspend its collapse into Mind, resulting in the No-Mind of *Third Attention*.

What becomes increasingly apparent through this tri-axial sequence of unfolding awareness is the illusion created by our perception. Lower down the spectrum our assumptions shape our perception of physical "reality"; whereas higher up the spectrum we lose all assumptions over our perceived "realities", and as a result we begin to see through the veil or beyond the doors of perception to the deeper Reality. However, rather than any lesser reality then disappearing in a "puff of smoke" as the illusion it is, such as this Physical World, it instead begins to glow with the radiance of the Reality we can perceive within its core. Our lower perception of this physical Life as a mess of Inertia, Desire and Fear transforms into a higher perception of the Goodness, Beauty and Truth it really is. The illusion is not that of perceiving form, but in not perceiving the radiant formlessness of form. It is only from an enlightened perspective that we can truly enjoy the illusion reality of this existence.

In the next Chapter we examine how all the states of phenomenal experience are actually perceived through the same simple Consciousness-Mind dynamic.

Chapter Eight

QUALIA AS A PRIMARY
AXIS DYNAMIC

W ITHOUT A MODEL of awareness that shows the dynamic of a Knower, a Means-of-knowing and the Known, it is hardly surprising that our Qualia, or experientially phenomenological states of awareness in a First Person context, are practically impossible to explain. But with a First Person model that does differentiate Consciousness and Mind as the Primary Axis, and also demonstrates how they operate in perception, the explanation of Qualia becomes surprisingly simple.

It has been discussed how the Three Tiers unfold when Consciousness, first identified and fused with Mind, then goes through Levels of dis-identification, gradually releasing itself through three Levels of Attention experienced as the Three Tiers. Next, the author proposes that *all Qualia can be explained in exactly the same way* – by the Attention operating in specified Tiers, and in specified conditions of engagement and disengagement, between the Subtle Consciousness and the Concrete Mind. The resulting perceptual shifts produce all known experiential states, or qualia, of Consciousness and Mind: waking, dreaming, lucid dreaming, deep sleep, deep absorption meditation, out-of-body and near-death experience, after-death experience and past life memories, mystical, hallucinogenic, hypnotic and delusional states.

In the *waking state* the Mind is in full physical (Concrete) awareness. In *First Tier*, Lower Mind assumes itself as the knower of phenomena and identifies with its thoughts, emotions and feelings. This is a result of the Mind being fused with Consciousness in a material identity we call Ego. But *in Second Tier,* when Consciousness differentiates from the Mind, the assumption accordingly shifts to Consciousness as the Knower of phenomena, with its Identity we call Soul. Its Higher Mind correlate accordingly assumes itself as the means of knowing. *In Third Tier,* the ever-awake Witness finally differentiates itself from Consciousness as the Supreme Knower of phenomena. Its Universal Mind, or Akasha, is its correlated Experience. In the Non-Dual state, Mind, Consciousness and Witness are Integral, as the One-Knower.

In *dreaming sleep* the Mind is in partial shutdown to allow its structures to metabolize its waking experience and is able to remember its dreams on waking. However, Consciousness *never* shuts down. *In First Tier,* if it is fused or over-identified with the Mind. Then it plays no part in dreaming sleep other than as a fused witness of the dreams. In this state the Conscious Identity is fluid and can change according to the dream. *In Second Tier,* the Conscious Self has differentiated itself and can witness and even participate in the Mind's dream in a state called *lucid dreaming* that has full conscious recall. In one lucid dream someone encountered a far-away friend, who was in Wales, in his dream. They went on a lucid journey together over Wales, visiting their favorite places. First thing the next morning the friend called him to tell him of that same dream, and to ask if he had experienced it! *In Third Tier,* lucid dreaming sleep is an Akashic experience of the Causal Mind.

In *deep sleep* there is total shutdown of the Mind. *In First Tier,* with a Consciousness fused or over-identified with Mind, the result is total unconsciousness with no recall of being asleep even though Consciousness is present as always. Sophisticated brain imaging has shown this to be the case, but without a model to explain it. *In Second Tier,* while the Mind is in shutdown, the Consciousness can enter states of deep absorption into Causal Consciousness, with total recall, as in *Third Tier.* Total recall is possible here because Causal Consciousness is at one with Causal Mind and its Akashic memory.

Deep absorption can also be entered with the waking Mind through meditation. Here the Mind is shut down intentionally by the Attention. The Attention then surrenders its hold on all lesser Consciousness identities until *there is only the Third Tier Knower* in Causal Consciousness. Again, total recall of deep absorption is possible because Causal Consciousness is not-two with Causal (Akashic) Mind.

In *near-death experience* (NDE) a trauma shuts down the Mind, leaving the Conscious identity in limbo and free to witness the transition from physical reality (such as the scene of an accident, and leaving one's body) to the non-physical reality of the after-death state, and finally the return back to one's body. There is a great amount of empirical evidence that comes with NDE's, when the brain and Mind flat-line. *In First Tier,* Mind and Consciousness remain fused and the result is an unconscious coma until reawakening. But *in Second Tier,* Consciousness is differentiated, self-aware, and free to witness the surrounding events, along with many commonalities such as entering a tunnel of light and entering non-material realms "beyond" the physical, all of which are remembered despite the flat-lined brain. *In Third Tier,* spontaneous Enlightenment can occur. This attests to the autonomy of non-local Consciousness from the local reality of the Body-Mind. A key article in this regard is by the heart surgeon Pim Van Lommel (2013) in the *Journal of Consciousness Studies,* with the following Abstract:

In this article a concept of Non-local Consciousness will be described, based on scientific research on Near Death Experiences (NDE's).

In *after-death experience,* the physical body and Lower Mind disintegrate, leaving the Consciousness free to experience and identify with after-life phenomena at the Level to which it has evolved. In *First Tier,* the process begins with the "death swoon" because Consciousness is fused with Lower Mind and lapses into unconsciousness when the Lower Mind disintegrates. It then reawakens in whatever after-death state, or Bardo, that corresponds to its Level of evolution, from where it chooses a correlated incarnation. In *Second Tier*, Consciousness is drawn to the its Causal State and is given the opportunity to let go into post-mortal Enlightenment. If it cannot, it retreats to whatever Bardo correlates to its Level of evolution until the time comes to choose a correlated incarnation. In *Third Tier*, Consciousness automatically merges with its Source in post-mortem Enlightenment. From the latter perspective of Continuous Consciousness between incarnations, accounts of the after-death state come from such Enlightened Souls as the Buddha, living Dalai Lamas and bhodisattvas, whose words carry great weight. A Dalai Lama consciously chooses the next reincarnation and is identified by the devotees who find the child by its ability to correctly identify possessions from the previous life. This is as empirical as it gets, and is dealt with in the next section.

Hallucinogenic states can also lead to out-of-body experiences and NDE's, following the same process where the hallucinogen aids in the differentiation of a fully-awake Consciousness from a fully-awake Mind, and where the resulting experience is Level-specific.

Mystical States happen when the differentiation of a fully awake Consciousness and Mind is spontaneous. Often, Consciousness operating at a temporarily higher Level than Mind induces the mystical state. The relative Levels involved between Consciousness and Mind results in correlated types of mystical experience. For example, a person whose cognition is in Red and has a spontaneous shift in Consciousness to Violet will experience everything in mystical awe. Cases of such spontaneous Enlightenment have resulted in psychological dysfunction through the disparity between an Ultra-Violet Consciousness having to operate through, for example, Green cognition.

Hypnotic states have a similar cause, where the hypnotist aids in the differentiation of a fully awake Consciousness from a fully awake Mind, and where the resulting experience is guided by the hypnotist's suggestion and interpreted according to the Level for the period of regression.

Delusional states such as Schizophrenia with multiple personalities usually happen at an early fulcrum arrest of the Mind (Octant

2) due to trauma, where the fused First Person Consciousness safely splits off the traumatized proximate "I" (Octant 1) as a compartmentalized distal "Me" (Octant 5), accompanied by "My" sub-personalities (Octant 6).

There are also *Mind States* and *Consciousness Structures.* First Person Mind States are our *felt-states* at All Levels of Mind, where feelings in both the experiential intelligence (Octant 2) and correlated personality (Octant 6) form a combined experience, positive or negative, be it anger, joy, hatred, love. First Person Consciousness Structures at All Levels are Non-Local, such as the Attention that stabilizes our position on the Spectrum (Octant 1), or the Intention as a behavioral motive of Consciousness (Octant 5).

From this brief survey it can be seen how such a very simple Primary Axis dynamic, as Levels of engagement and disengagement between the Subtle Consciousness and the Concrete Mind, can produce and explain such an immense complexity of awareness.

Chapter Nine

INCARNATE
AND DISINCARNATE
EXISTENCE

T HE DIRECT IMPLICATION of the various states of Consciousness and Mind we have just discussed is the continuity of Consciousness awareness after the dissolution of the physical Body-Mind in death, and even from life to life. In this book, rather than try to prove a case for the Afterlife, or the Between-lives, we pursue explanations for existing evidence via our central hypothesis of a dynamic between the Subtle Consciousness and the Concrete Mind in their correlated Spectrums.

In ancient Tibet the deep-absorption meditators were so adept at going into the after-life realms that they compiled a detailed experiential map of after-death states that became *The Tibetan Book of the Dead*. They called the after-death realms "Bardos", which reflected the surviving Consciousness of the deceased and the experience of which determined the nature and circumstances of the next birth. An unbroken continuity of Consciousness as recommended by the Buddha led to the best rebirth. For example, the next Dalai Lama is empirically chosen by his ability to remember his previous life as Dalai Lama. Objects either precious or significant to him in that life have to be identified by the new incarnation.

The Idealist view of this is that we each of us are a Consciousness Monad, an evolving entity with our own agenda, similar to the

Christian "Soul". Our cognitive evolution in the Concrete Domain is dis-continuous from life to life, each time beginning at birth at the bottom of the cognitive Ladder. On the other hand, the evolution of our Subtle Consciousness as Climber is continuous. The implication here is that our Consciousness intends our incarnation, and that our rebirth therefore has perfect continuity whether we remember the process or not, as Buddha attested to in his "Continuity of Consciousness".

So the traditional evolutionary debates, even in Integral circles, about the evolution of physical forms are extremely one-sided. Even Wilber's "First Tier" AQAL Square, in making no allowance for the co-evolution of the Subtle Consciousness monad, has to try to explain the physical evolution of Life-forms in the vague spiritual terminology of "Eros" and "Agape" drives, or evolutionary/involutionary drives, which advance the debate no further than any other Primum Mobile "explanation".

The Primary Axis injunction clarifies this completely, in that the involution of the Subtle Consciousness monad and its evolving Concrete incarnations *are* the Agape and Eros drives. The more the Subtle Consciousness gets involved in its Concrete Life, the more its Life and Mind get evolved in a capacity for Consciousness. This Primary Axis dynamic can easily explain such phenomena as child prodigies and genius, when an evolved Consciousness monad incarnates and "fast tracks" its cognitive development to the Level achieved in its previous life.

The situation is somewhat like a driver (Consciousness) and the car (Body) with its software (Mind). The driver is independent of the car, in that cars are disposable, but the driver is also dependent on the car in order to evolve as a driver. As the driver evolves, so the cars become more powerful, computerized and complex. Race drivers commonly redesign and re-engineer their own cars, as a result of their own experience and insight, to improve performance. This co-evolution implies the integral necessity of a physical incarnation or Life to ultimately attain the Grand Prix of Consciousness – Enlightenment. Also implied is that when the driver gets out of the car or when the car falls apart along with all its onboard software the driver, Consciousness, moves on to a newer, faster car.

Our Consciousness has an Enlightenment imperative, an evolutionary need to resolve its identity issues and at last be atoned to its undifferentiated state. It expresses this need by intending an incarnation to best satisfy that need. Consciousness is the seat of our Intent, which is colored and clouded by whatever band of the Spectrum we identify with – the joys and sorrows, attractions and repulsions, the loves and hates to be found on those Levels of identification. The Ancient Traditions claim that these karmic formations, or *skandhas*, are the templates of our intention for an incarnation best suited to deal with them, so that our droplet may best find its stream, then its river to the ocean. The stream of life flows with this perfect, coherent, evolving continuity of identity from Id to Ego to Soul to Supreme Witness.

In other words, our Consciousness intends its incarnation into this Concrete Domain to best pursue its evolutionary objectives. This may seem shocking to us, especially if our life has been beset by trials and tribulations. But those very trials could be what we actually need in order to wake up into Consciousness. Eventually, our Enlightenment imperative becomes fully conscious, and we begin to "remember", we begin to wake up.

We discussed how the psychological Structure Stages are like a ladder and in any one life the ladder of Structure Stages must be reclimbed from the very first rung. No rung can be skipped any more than a floor can be skipped in the construction of a building. So in terms of the Mind's Structure Stages we are all born equal on the ground floor, or first rung of the Ladder. But we did not discuss the Climber of the Ladder – how the identity stage of our Subtle Consciousness also evolves over lifetimes, but with continuity.

In our evolving Consciousness we are *not* all born as equal. Because of our individual karmic agenda, in our Consciousness we can be more of a "novice Soul", or an "old Soul", than those around us. The higher the State Stage of our incarnating Consciousness, the faster we can evolve through our incarnate Mind's Structure Stages. This is because we are able to intend better and better births conducive to our evolution. Child prodigies and precocious development can be explained by an advanced Consciousness "fast-tracking" its Cognitive development. For example, there is abundant footage on You Tube of the spiritual master Prem Rawat at the age of three warming up the crowds assembled for his father, a well-known guru in India who was also Prem's master. At the age of nine, Prem succeeded his father as an Enlightenment teacher, and first came to teach in the West when he was thirteen years old. He is still going strong forty five years later, and has garnered numerous humanitarian awards for his efforts as an "Ambassador of Peace", and in the relief of human suffering.

The continuity of Consciousness is therefore seamlessly perfect. Our drop eventually slips into the sea, but the sea can also slip into our drop at any point along the way, according to our thirst for the ocean. In his book *The Physics Of The Soul* (2001), Amit Goswami provides a quantum explanation of reincarnation in describing our individual Consciousness, our own "drop", as an evolving entity called the Quantum Monad. What makes each of us unique as a Quantum Monad is the perspective or position we occupy on the Spectrum of Consciousness, as a result of the choices we make in our journey back to the Source.

Dr. Ian Stephenson (1987) pioneered the accumulation of empirical evidence of past life memory in a now iconic body of work, where the subjects, usually children, remember the locations of their previous lives and interact with people they used to know.

But the most rigorous empirical experiments regarding actual Subtle disincarnate existence have been done by Dr. Gary Schwartz (2002) of the University of Arizona at the Human Energy Systems Laboratory. Through a series of rigorous double blind experiments he had a number of reputable psychics and mediums individually contact one named deceased entity per experiment, with living relatives accessible for cross-confirmation under extremely isolated and insulated conditions He asked the same list of personal and intimate questions. In most experiments the psychics and mediums averaged

80% unanimity. These experiments are ongoing to determine whether Subtle conscious existence is parallel with physical Concrete existence.

The Afterlife Experiments beg the question of how the Subtle Consciousness extends its agenda into Concrete Life. It is not only a question of how we choose our next incarnation, but also how our Subtle Consciousness actually meshes with and forms our Concrete Mind. This involutionary/evolutionary dynamic is called Volution, which we deal with in the next Chapter.

Chapter Ten

VOLUTION AS A PRIMARY AXIS DYNAMIC

T HE EVOLUTIONARY DEBATE, both in the conventional *and* the Integral arenas, is limited to the evolution of physical forms and their cognitive development - until Upper Second Tier for Integral Theory. "Wilber 5" allows for the subtle Soul to "emerge into existence" in Indigo; but this view is exclusive of *all* life forms except those few humans in Indigo and above; and it is also very one-sided when we consider the possibility that *all* evolving Concrete life forms are powered and operated by their evolving Subtle Consciousness monads from life to life.

We have seen how our evolving awareness is a two-way process between the Subtle Consciousness-Self and the Concrete Mind-Self, as driver and car. As Consciousness gets more and more involved in its physical life on the one hand, the correlated Mind gets more and more evolved into Consciousness on the other. This co-involution/evolution dynamic is called Volution, which is a holistic model of kosmic manifestation presented by Peter Merry (2012) in a paper by the same title. He indicates that as we involve so we evolve, immediately feeding back the evolutionary information we acquire back into the system.

A Vector Equilibrium is six pairs of vectors, six polarities holding the structure in balance... "It is literally a process of the integration of heaven and earth, of in-formation, as subtle energy potential inspires ("breathes into") physical form and physical form draws down the energy through its density and gravity so it can manifest in three-dimensional reality... "Seeing the Spiral in this way, as an example of a deeper creation dynamic, links it very closely to the dynamics of the torus. It is essentially a spinning dynamic... Ultimately then we can look at the human story more in terms of spin, pulses and breath, rather than linear evolution. It was this realisation, that evolution and involution are both part of the core life process, and that it is neither one without the other, that triggered me to use the term "volution" instead... "If we are to adopt the perspective of volution as the framework for our understanding of the life story, the great question remains: what is it that triggers disequilibrium in the unified field, leading to a collapse within the (Vector Equilibrium), toroidial spin dynamics and the localized manifestation of a life form? What creates life?...

Marshall Lefferts shared how the quantum level is what bridges the unified field and manifest reality. So the trigger must be related to the quantum field. He also shared how it is our consciousness that impacts this quantum level. The implications are that it is consciousness that can trigger the emergence of a life process through influencing probability in the quantum field. "In-tention" literally means bringing something into tension and as we know from the above, creative tension leads to manifestation. Conscious intention creates form – very literally in the form of sacks of manure and garden tools in the Perelandra context (Small Wright 1997) I understand the process as conscious intention bringing waves of potential into coherence, and exerting a pull in the unified field which sets off the process of volution. Arthur Young stated "The universe is a process put in motion by purpose.".

Rudolf Steiner made a similar formulation: *Imagine what you desire, will what you imagine, and create what you will.* If we equate *desire* with Attention, imagination with Intention, and *will* with Extension, it is as if to say that the purpose or Intent of our Subtle Consciousness is to evolve our Concrete Life to its fullest Extent. Instead of Body/Mind creating Consciousness, it is the other way around. Volution posits that the Subtle Consciousness acts through the Concrete Mind to manipulate genetic templates, using fundamental Concrete energies - variously called Quanta (New Physics),Morphic Resonance (Sheldrake), Psi (Radin), Chi (Chinese) and Prana (Hindu) - and thereby processes its Subtle Consciousness agenda into a living reality. This completely obviates the "Hard Problem" of how the brain generates its awareness. How is this?

To go back to Wilber's treatment of "subtle energies", which we now re-evaluate as "fundamental Concrete energies", he calls for their emergence from the Zero Point quantum vacuum as *Prana*. These are the energetic correlates of the experiential Mind, and their information is processed as experiential cognitive structures. As our cognitive experience evolves through the spectrum, the more complex our cognitive structures become, and the more fundamental the Concrete energies are required for their experiential processing. This is in compliance with Planck's Law – that the more fundamental the energy, the higher its frequency and the more information it contains.

Also, the higher the cognitive structures are on the spectrum of Mind, the more complex the correlated neurological structures become in the brain, with exponentially more synapses for processing the information available. In other words, the brain of a "saint" is far more neurologically complex than that of a "sinner". This increasing complexity also applies to Artificial Intelligence, where the high-speed processing of a quantum computer is prerequisite for high frequency/high information energy at the quantum-level.

However, we have seen how volution tells an additional story through experientially exponential feedback: as we move up the Ladder of Cognitive structures, experienced in First Person as Mind, we simultaneously open the valve at Zero Point to more and more *Prana* for powering the exponential of information involved, as per Planck's Law. Volving in this way can be with a *Prana* based meditation, from the Zero Point of *unconscious low quantum frequency Prana* at one end of the Concrete Spectrum to *super-conscious high quantum frequency Prana* at the opposite end.

In *The Primacy of Consciousness* (2014) Erwin Laszlo says:

Quantum theory offers further clues as to the nature of energy. The quantum is commonly called a quantum of energy, the smallest possible unit of energy. But that is not strictly correct. The quantum is actually a quantum of action. What is action? It is another physical quantity like distance, velocity, momentum, force, and others that we meet in physics, but it is not usually given much attention in our basic math or physics.

The amount of action in a quantum is exceedingly small, about 0.0 000000000000000000000000662618 erg.secs (or 6.62618 x 10 erg. secs in mathematical shorthand)—but it is always exactly the same amount. It is one of the few absolutes in existence, and more fundamental than space, time, matter, or energy. The Zero-Point Field is not therefore a potential energy field—despite the fact it is often referred to as such. It is a potential quantum field, a field of potential action...

Note: we must clarify here that the Zero Point Field is the Local "ground of being" for this Physical Universe, which the Tibetans call *Thigle*, meaning "the dense place"; but it is *not* the Kosmic Ground of Being, which is the Primordial Vibration of Energy.

Within the context of "fundamental Concrete energies", what is actually going on here? Planck's law basically states that information, as the action potential of energy, is in direct proportion to frequency; or the higher its frequency, the more information energy can encode. So Zero Point Field *Prana* at the level of "unconscious quantum simplicity" is modulating at a relatively low frequency compared to *Prana* at the level of "super-conscious quantum complexity". As the frequency of Conscious awareness elevates through the Subtle spectrum, it induces a correlated elevated frequency modulation of *Prana*, and therefore of Mind, in the Concrete spectrum. Frequencies beyond 80 Hz are well attested to in experiments with meditators, while "normal" is below 40 Hz.

In other words, the process of evolving through our cognitive structures is the process of involving more and more *Prana/Kundalini* into our being from our Root Chakra to our Crown Chakra, as we move through the spectrum of awareness. Clearly in this context the Chakras serve as portal interfaces between our Subtle and Concrete awareness, whereby Subtle information as Intention can be transduced by Extension into correlated Levels of Concrete awareness and energetic enactment. This is discussed in the next chapter.

Earlier we discussed how the Subtle and Concrete spectrums are like the UHF and VHF Bands of a radio. Using that analogy we are now in a position to see that the seven Chakras are the transducers of at least seven such full-spectrum Frequency Bands, the lower four pertaining to the Concrete Domain, the middle two to the Subtle Domain and the highest one to the Causal Domain. Each of these Bands gives us a different awareness, a different worldview, which we tune into as we evolve. But because each Chakra *is* full spectrum, the Base Chakra of a "saint" has a much higher vibration than that of a "sinner", and as a result a "saint" has no attachment or survival issues!

The author proposes that our First, Second, Third and Fourth Person awareness we have of this Concrete Domain are the result of the first four Chakras coming "on line"; that our Fifth and Sixth Person awareness are the result of our Subtle Chakras coming on "on line"; and that our Seventh Person awareness is the result of our Causal (Crown) Chakra coming "on line". "On line" means emerging into our awareness, rather than emerging into existence. For example, a baby in First Person cognition also has awareness of mama (Second Person) and also of milk (Third Person), but they are all experientially fused in a First Person oneness and not yet differentiated as self-aware First Person, self-aware Second Person and self-aware Third Person. At the other end, when our Soul-self (Sixth Person) emerges into self-awareness around Indigo, we have the realization that our Soul-self has been there all along from our earliest existence without our knowing it.

First Person awareness begins with the identification of survival needs – the Id identity. Second Person awareness is relating to those who attend to our needs, and the lower Ego. Third Person awareness relates to the world at large that satisfies all our material needs, and the self- aware Ego. Fourth Person awareness cares for that world, dis-identifying with material needs, and the autonomous Ego. Fifth Person awareness identifies with our Subtle-self as Consciousness. Sixth Person awareness identifies as our Subtle Soul in becoming aware of our Causal-self as Witness. Seventh Person awareness dis-identifies with Consciousness, as the Supreme Witness or One Knower. Clearly, therefore, the Persons as experiential worldviews are the experiential effects of the Chakras processing those levels of self-awareness.

It now becomes apparent why all the **Persons** operate with all Eight Fundamental Perspectives, because the Chakras process all Eight Fundamental Perspectives. We discuss this further in the next chapter.

In Chapter 4 we saw in the Cubic Die cosmology how the Chakras operate in pairs via the breath spiral. We are now in a position to understand how volution operates, as both involving and evolving Breath/ Chi/Prana/Psi, via the higher and lower Chakra pairs. In other words, the expansion of our awareness is not linearly from the lower to higher Chakras, but as a volutionary resonance **between** the lower and higher Chakras. The Chakras are therefore the Subtle-to-Concrete transducers and processors of the in-formation that forms our awareness. Then how is this information processed within the Chakras?

At the forefront of empirical research in non-locality is that of Torsional Waves at the Zero Point Field, shown in Figure 25. Torsional Wave modulation is proving to be the means of encoding and transduction of information between the Subtle and Concrete spectrums. Quantum teleportation experiments show that Torsional Waves as carriers of information are not limited by the speed of light, but that they travel with instantaneity.

Nassim Haramein, Director of Research at the Hawaii Institute for Unified Physics, has modeled the transduction of information via Torsional Waves over the local/non-local interface (2004). His model of this transducer is a quantum Torsional Wave vortex that has the fundamental form of a star tetrahedron – two inter-locking

Figure 25. A Torsional Wave

tetrahedrons like a three-dimensional Solomon's Seal (shown in Figure 26). The tetrahedron is the most fundamental three-dimensional form, and as such can structurally operate at a fundamental quantum unit level of energy at the Planck scale.

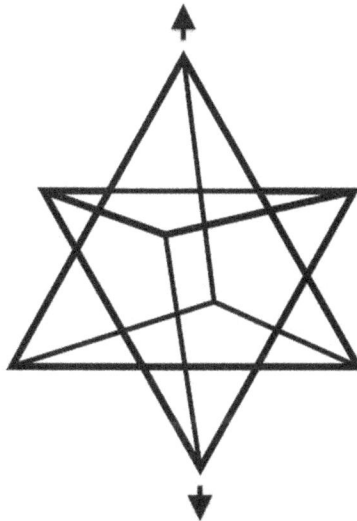

Figure 26. Haramein's Interlocking Tetrahedrons As An Energy Quantum

Haramein actually describes this double-tetrahedron structure as a double-torus, creating a feedback loop vortex by which information is processed in a state of quantum resonance, as similarly described by the torsional wave model. Torsional waves have tension, torque and torsion. Tension can compress or dilate the frequency of a wave, so that an in-tension can transfer information from one Band *Frequency* to another. Torque is force, which can encode the intensity or *Amplitude* of an intention. And torsion is the ability of a wave to travel out of or in to Space-time according to its *Polarity*, thereby removing or imposing limits on its velocity from infinite to finite.

Our Subtle Consciousness resonating in the "UHF Band" of Figure 26 downloads correlated information into our Concrete Mind resonating in the "VHF Band", and vice versa; where an *encoded Intent* is transduced as Extent, the result of which is transduced back in a torus feedback loop. In the next Chapter we explore the possible mechanism behind this transduction of information.

Chapter Eleven

DECODING QUANTUM PERSPECTIVES

T HE TRANSDUCTION AND translation of information from one form of energy to another requires a transcription code. An insight into such a Quantum code comes from a web paper by Charles Higgins, *"The Quantum State of Alchemy"*. By "Alchemy" he is making the association between Quantum States and Quantum Mind, and alchemically he deduces the Eight Fundamental Perspectives:

> *The **Quantum State** is the complementation of three different binary lines. As an example, using the three binary lines, luminosity, humidity, and temperature, this complementation produces a three-dimensional model with the binary lines now labeled **p, q** and **m**...*
>
> *Instead of four elements as in the First Complement State, the Quantum State has eight elements. Each one of these eight elements is a complementation of active or inactive elements from the three binary lines. The eight elements of the example are light-dry-warm, light-dry-cold, light-moist-warm, dark-dry-warm, dark-moist-warm, dark-dry-cold, light-moist-cold and dark-moist-cold.*
>
> *The equation for this 3-dimensional model is derived in a similar manner as the two-dimensional equation. Each element in the Quantum State is a quantum field more simply called an octant...*
>
> *The algebraic and symbolic notation for the eight quantum fields is shown by their different combinations of bold and thin lines.*

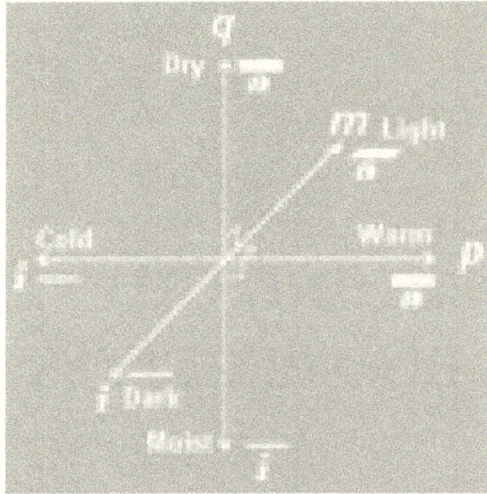

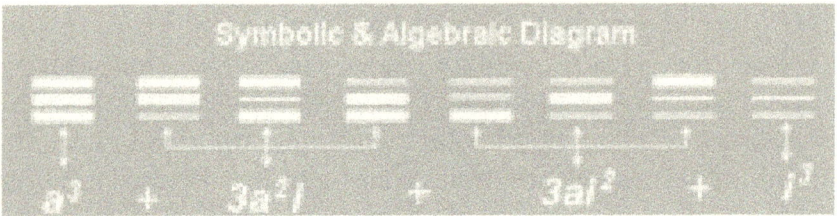

Symbolic & Algebraic Diagram

$$a^3 + 3a^2i + 3ai^2 + i^3$$

The diagram above also shows the algebraic summation of the eight quantum fields. This summation can be shown by the dimensional equation, and by factoring this summed equation we arrive at the general equation for the three- dimensional or Quantum State.

I CHING CORRELATION

The eight quantum fields of the ether discussed above correspond to the trigrams of the I Ching as shown below.

$$f(m_s) = a^3 + 3a^2i + 3ai^2 + i^3$$

$$f(m_s) = (a + i)_p \times (a + i)_m \times (a + i)_q$$

$$f(m_s) = (a + i)^3$$

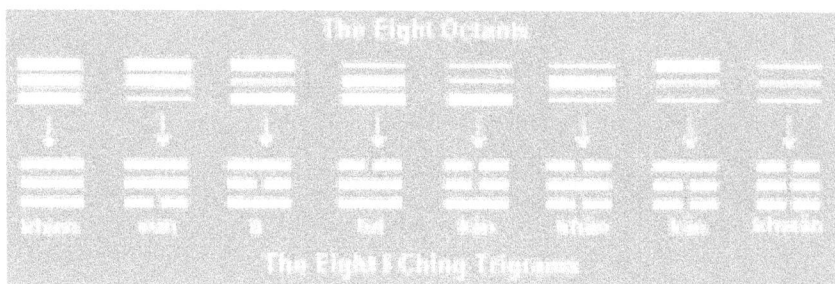

In this Eight Perspectives model, Higgins discusses the correlation between the Eight Trigram Perspectives and the eight quantum fields, as eight quantum triplets, exactly like the AQAL Cube model. The eight quantum fields are discussed in the next chapter, but suffice to say here that quantum physics differentiates four fundamental forces operating through four fundamental particles as the basis of all subatomic particles. If Higgins' hypothesis that the eight quantum fields serve as a code for information is correct, then Haramein's Torsional Wave star-tetrahedron mechanism for transducing information across the Zero Point Field could serve as a simple means to encode that information as the Eight Fundamental Perspectives.

The *I Ching*'s 64 Hexagrams, as binary permutations of its 8 x 8 Trigram Perspectives, are therefore binary perspectives. We have seen how taking any perspective is actually a binary perspective between a subject/observer and object/observed. Perception is therefore a self-referential system of perspectives taking perspectives.

Given that a conscious perspective is Level-specific, then a binary perspective between any two perspectives forms a lattice of possible All-Level permutations formed by the two perspectives, shown in Figure 27. Looking at that generic binary perspective lattice of All-Level permutations, a balanced development of that binary perspective through the Levels would be fairly straight down the middle; but the development of a binary perspective is rarely so direct, and normally veers between extremes before getting it right.

For example, a classic scenario of such a wobbling binary perspective is the disparity between our self-image, of how we see our-

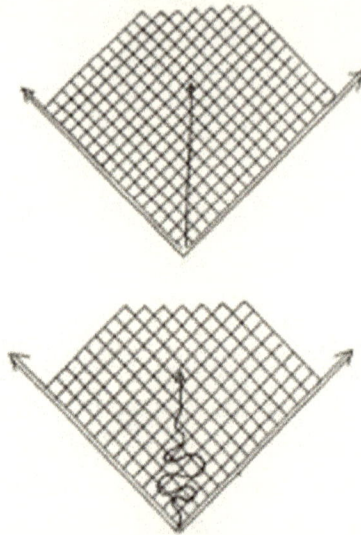

Figure 27. The Development Of a Generic Binary Perspective.

selves as a Persona (Octant 5), and our behavioral-self as a Personality (Octant 6). We usually rate our self-image much higher than our actual personality bears out, resulting in hubris-to-humility scenarios.

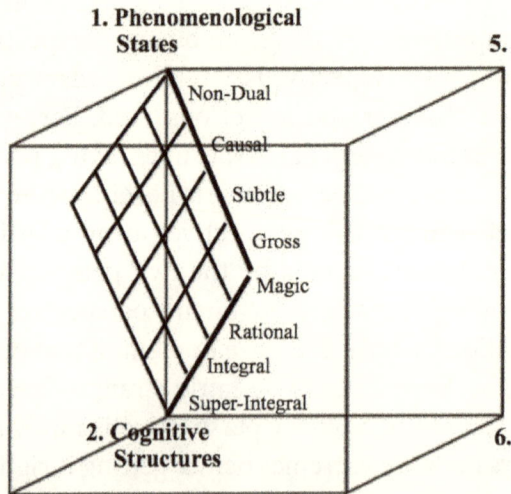

Figure 28. An AQAL Cube Binary-Perspective Lattice.

In the classic Wilber-Combs Lattice correlating Consciousness States and Cognitive Structures there are 16 such permutations through 4 x 4 Levels. In Figure 28 the W-C Lattice correlates Consciousness States and Cognitive Structures between Perspectives #1 and #2 on the AQAL Cube.

Figure 29 shows the AQAL Cube with a total of 32 Binary Perspective Lattices off its 12 edges, 12 diagonals and 8 Vertex-Nodes, giving 64 reversed perspective lattices exactly like the *I Ching*'s 64 Hexagrams.

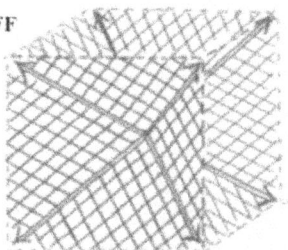

LATTICES OFF

12 EDGES

LATTICES OFF

12 DIAGONALS

Figure 29. AQAL Cube Binary Perspective Lattices off 12 edges and 12 diagonals:

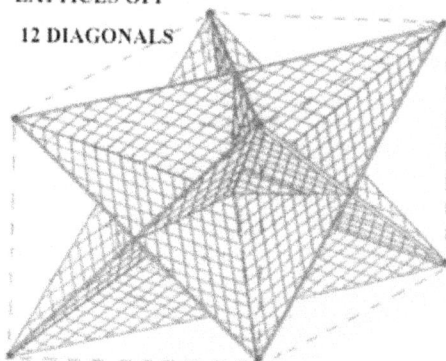

The above AQAL Cube binary perspective lattices form a **star-tetrahedron,** which Nassim Haramein describes as a quantum transduction vortex, a resonating star-tetrahedron generated by torsional waves at the Planck scale, shown in Figure 26. The irony here is that the fabled *Planck's Cube* holds a fundamental quantum unit of energy, as does *Haramein's star tetrahedron*. It would therefore seem that the *AQAL Cube*, as an Eight Fundamental Perspectives model, doubles as Planck's Cube *and* Haramein's quantum transducer – meaning that *the AQAL Cube is possibly both a cosmological model and a structure* at the quantum level. The author's ongoing research is in the direction of validating the AQAL Cube as a quantum model *and* structure at the core of Concrete and Subtle manifestation.

Haramein's work in this field is indeed confirming a fundamental quantum geometry that operates through the Platonic solid structures, particularly the tetrahedron, the cube, the star-tetrahedron, the octahedron and the dodecahedron. These solids expand on each other in a natural unfolding sequence of geometric complexity. Haramein confirms Plato's prediction of how matter from the most fundamental quantum state unfolds in complexity. A paper presented by Haramein (2008) at the Unified Theories Conference actually discusses the structural geometry existing at the quantum scale (the bold emphases are the author's):

> In this paper, we have **developed a scaling law for the universal, galactic, stellar-solar and atomic scale frequencies vs. radius of the system**, with the consideration of a fundamental response of these systems within the surrounding structured vacuum polarization...
>
> **The octahedron** and **the cube** have the same symmetry group and are dual to each other under the S4 group. **The icosahedron** and the **dodecahedron** are dual to each other under the A5 group and the 12-element group T is the **tetrahedral group** of which the symmetries are inscribed in S2 and is the A4 group. The 24 element **octahedral group** is denoted as O and is the set of all symmetries inscribed in S2 , which is also the **symmetry group of the cube** since **the six faces of the cube correspond to the six vertices of the octahedron and eight faces of the octahedron correspond to the eight vertices of the cube.** The relationship of the finite and infinitesimal groups is key to understanding the symmetry relation of particles, matter and force fields or gauge fields and the structural topology of space, i.e. real, complex and abstract spaces. **We now relate the toroidal topology and the cuboctahedron geometry to current particle physics...**

The eight (8) fundamental spinor states can be expressed in terms of the Riemann sphere S2 which defines the relationship of spinors to space-time. The 8 spinor states correspond to the 8 vertices of a cube...

"As before stated, the cube and octahedron are dual to each other under the symmetry operations of the S4 group. Also, the tetrahedron has the alternate A4 group, and the icosahedron and dodecahedron are dual under the A5 group...

The relationship of the cuboctahedral groups and the dual torus is a fundamental tenant of the Haramein geometric topology and, as seen here, seems to be fundamental for unification.

In other words, Haramein has simplified the description of complex energy resonance at the quantum level using geometric structures that hold the toroidal and torsional fields. For example a Cube, while holding a Star Tetrahedron at its eight vertices as 12 diagonal perspective lattices, is similarly held by a Rhombic Dodecahedron at the same eight vertices as 12 edge perspective lattices. The Rhombic Dodecahedron is an everted Cube along its 12 edges. Remembering Fig. 29 showing all the binary perspective lattices generated by a Cube from 12 diagonals and 12 edges, we now expand those perspective lattices to a new order of permutations as a 12 –faced Rhombic Dodecahedron, shown in Figure 30.

Bearing in mind that the Star Tetrahedron is nested in the Cube, and the Cube everts to a Rhombic Dodecahedron, we can see that quantum connectivity and processing is really a state of resonance between these fundamental structures. For example, the lattices of adjacent cubes are not so much connected face to face but by the rhombic lattices of the Rhombic Dodecahedrons that the Cubes are nested in. The nested tetrahedron/cube/dodecahedron structures are in reality processors of quantum information that is energetically encoded in, and shared by, their binary perspective lattices. A binary perspective lattice correlates the spectrums of two perspectives, as a binary perspective. The information encoded increases exponentially towards the higher end of the spectrum.

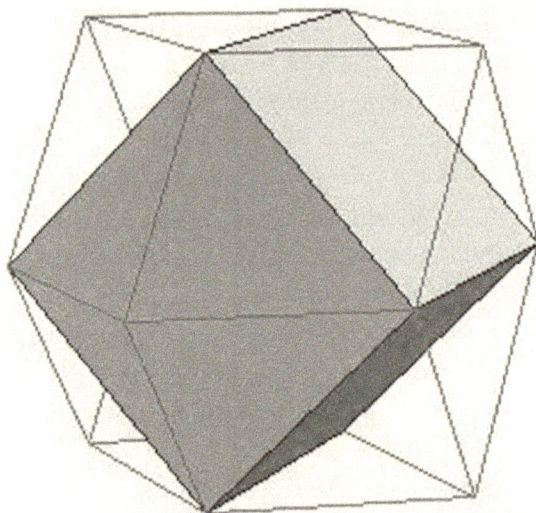

Figure 30. Rhombic Dodecahedron As 6 Pyramids Of An Everted Cube

So the question remains, how do these perspective lattices translate an encoded conscious Subtle Intent into a correlated Concrete Extent? In other words, how does the information get translated from a "UHF" band to a "VHF" band?

Heisenberg's Uncertainty Principle shows that the very act of taking a conscious perspective binds the observer participant and observed as a binary perspective lattice, in a Consciousness-Mind-Energy continuum we now call entanglement. We have seen how entanglement is effected by torsional waves, as information bridges. The inference here is that torsional wave transduction can encode perspectival information as an energetic lattice of 64 codon permutations per quantum torsional unit, which are generated as the "Eight Spinor States" described by Haramein, and encoded as Eight Fundamental Codon-triplets shown in Figure 31.

We described previously how the Chakras are Torsional Wave interfaces, as information bridges between the Three Domains. It now becomes apparent that Haramein's "eight spinor states" may provide the basis of the eight codon triplets, which process information via their correlated Chakras as the Eight Fundamental Perspectives, as in Figure 32. In this context Haramein's quantum geometric structures

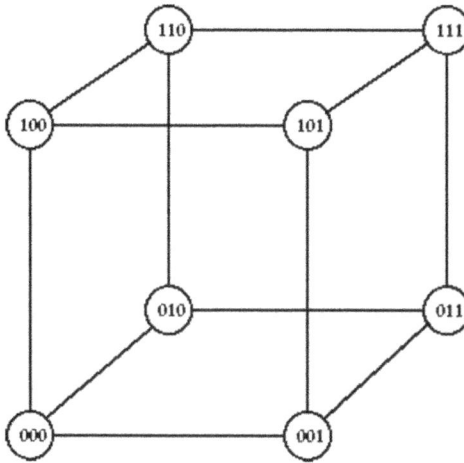

Figure 31. The Eight Quantum Codons As 0-1 Polarity Triplets.

are micro-processors of quantum information, and the Chakras are the macro-processors. If so, then this mechanism demonstrates how the Chakras provide the experiential basis of Mind.

In the New Physics scientists like Nassim Haramein are showing how energy in torsion, torque and torus spins a yarn out of "nothing", which can then be woven into the fabric of physical existence. How-

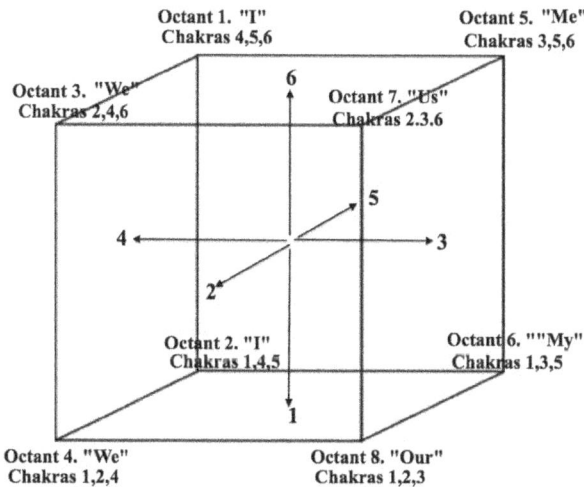

Figure 32. The Eight First Person Perspectives as Correlated Chakras

ever, energy is energy whether a non-local "nothing" or a local "something", the difference determined by the modulations of its amplitude, frequency and polarity as a waveform. It is the torsion, torque and torus of energy, as forces that modulate the amplitude, frequency and polarity of the wave, that determine its form emerging at the quantum scale. In his Unified Description of Nature (2010), Peter Jakubowski posits a simple equation that shows how the very first proto-state of matter emerges from the Quantum Field as a fundamental "fluctuon" (f) through a quantum wave vector (k) at a propagation velocity (c). Which begs the question: what generates the propagation forces?

To answer this, New Physics turns from Energy to Consciousness. If *Energia* is "at work", then who is the worker? We have seen how Energy and Consciousness are two sides of the same coin. Consciousness applies force as Intent. The Intent is encoded by torsion, torque and torus, and applied into Extent through a quantum form with amplitude, frequency and polarity. In other words Intent opens a "wormhole" of torsion, torque and torus into the arena of Extent. On a macrocosmic scale the Intent to form a galaxy of star-systems opens up a galactic black hole from which all pours forth. At one time it was thought to be the other way around – a galaxy forms a black hole at its core; but Haramein's calculations (2013) show that *everything* from the macrocosmic to the microcosmic Planck scale is formed around black holes, even at the core of a proton, where a black hole is a non-local to local portal.

Which brings us to Chakras, wheels of energy vortices like mini-galaxies, funneling our Conscious Intent into the Extent of our human form and its activity as a Consciousness-Mind-Energy continuum. The context usually applied to the Chakras is an energy field upholding our physical existence like a bubble in the ocean depths. But more to the point they provide the field of awareness where our Consciousness interfaces with Mind. This correctly implies that the brain and neural system are mere organic delegators, providing the physical means to interpret and bodily enact the Intent.

We have seen how the six Chakras, as Mind, rather than operating individually as a sequential hierarchy operate *together* in a resonant holarchy, or a sequential wholeness of paired polarities 1-6, 2-5,

3-4. Through the breath cycle this holarchic integration becomes a self-aware process, at which point breath awareness expands exponentially as Spirit awareness, or more specifically as the expansion of Consciousness and Mind.

As a result, the Eight Fundamental Perspectives also expand, where each Perspective is a function of the three Chakras comprising that Perspective. For example, our most Concrete Perspective is Octant 8, or how we participate socially in the energy environment, operating through the three "below-the-belt" Chakras 1, 2, 3. Our most Subtle Perspective is diametrically opposite, Octant 1, or our proximate self awareness, operating through the three "above-the-belt" Chakras 4, 5, 6.

If each Fundamental Perspective is formed as a resonance between the three participating Chakras, then any contraction in a given Chakra, such as Fear in the Third Chakra, will result in a correlated contraction of any Perspective operating through the Third Chakra. So an initial therapy would be to bring the Third Chakra in resonance with its polarity – the Heart Chakra. Breath awareness will do this, but also in conjunction with Fourth Chakra functions such as empathy and compassion for the fear in others. The Crown Chakra is the prime integrator of the Consciousness/Mind dynamic because it is the seat of our awareness as the All-Domain, All-Quadrant, All-Level Witness.

In other words, our Chakras are the basis of our experiential awareness as Mind and not the brain/neural complex. Experiential quantum processing of information as an Intent is given Extent through the Chakras as Mind, which then informs the brain/neural complex to act on the Intent. This being the case, how would a proto-organism perceive, orient itself, navigate and function in its environment? In his *EnlighteNext* interview Hameroff explains concisely how non-local Consciousness finds quantum locality in an organism:

...(Penrose) suggested that consciousness is the wave-function collapse, or at least one particular kind of collapse. It's a quantum collapse that gives off fundamental units of conscious awareness, just

like an electron orbital shift gives off a photon of light. And like pho-
tons, quanta of consciousness come in a spectrum of different intensi-
ties, frequencies and qualities...
"In Roger's model, which he calls orchestrated objective reduction,
you don't always need an outside observer. If a quantum system
evolves to a critical threshold – which involves gravitational warping
on the quantum scale – it will self-collapse. There's an objective, natu-
ral reduction of the quantum wave function that results in a simple
moment of consciousness, or a simple "quantum" of consciousness, if
you will. And when these collapses happen again and again in your
brain, you get a series of conscious moments that give rise to your
experience of a stream of consciousness. So consciousness, in this
model, consists of a series of discrete events, yet is experienced as con-
tinuous. You can think of it kind of as frames in a movie, only with a
movie you have an outside observer. In this case, the frame itself has
the observer built into it. The conscious moment and the quantum
wave-function collapse are one and the same event.

So the question regarding an organism's perception, orientation, navigation and function in the environment is really about how the information contained in an organism's non-local Intention gets transcribed into a correlated local action, via that wave-function collapse (better described as Jakubowski's "fluctuon" or Haramein's toroidal transduction at the Planck scale).

Any physically embodied organism transcribes its "Inside" to "Outside" experience via molecular codes. Once again, these molecular codes are rooted in the Eight Fundamental Perspectives using 8 x 8 = 64 recombinant permutations. The most famous transcription code of all, the genetic code, enables an organism to evolve according to its own innovative needs via a DNA code of four basic amino acids in a double-recombinant format of 64 permutations per molecular unit.

The implications here are self-evident, where an organism's individual need (Intention), in the "UHF" band, is encoded by the proposed quantum unit of 64 codons in a correlated "VHF" band, which can then torsion-induce the *correlated* mutation in its own 64 permutation DNA molecular unit to meet that need. So, it would appear that two equally basic and intermeshing 8 x 8 = 64 transcription codes, one quantum and the other molecular, could enable an organism's Subtle Consciousness to intend an infinite complexity of Concrete effects, via quantum Mind, to a correlated cellular action. We are talking about Haramein's "eight spinor states" embodying a transcription code at the most fundamental quantum ("fluctuon") level that could quantify the Eight Fundamental Perspectives. How can this be done?

The quintessential properties of any torsional waveform, as a vibration, are Amplitude, Frequency and Polarity. A simple example of this are the three modes of radio Bands: Amplitude Modulation (AM), Frequency Modulation (FM) and Digital or Polarity Modulation. I therefore propose the possibility that each of the Eight Fundamental Perspectives of the AQAL Cube can be encoded at the most fundamental level, *as a quantum-triplet*, through torsional vibration on three axes: *Amplitude* (Large/Small), *Frequency* (High/Low), and *Polarity* (Spin), or *AFP*.

In the *EnlighteNext* interview, Hameroff continues:

We know that consciousness in the brain happens at about forty times per second. It's called gamma synchrony... And in the model that Roger [Penrose, collaborator] and I have developed, we've proposed that Singer's gamma synchrony is actually evidence of quantum-state collapses happening forty times per second – or more – among coherent, organized networks of the brain's microtubules...

And a few years ago, the Dalai Lama sent some of his best meditators to a lab up in Wisconsin. They found that, while meditating, the monks had the highest gamma synchrony ever recorded. They were actually operating at about eighty to one hundred hertz, whereas the experimental control subjects were at forty... Years of meditating had changed their brains so that they were just normally in this higher-frequency gamma range. That suggests they're having a richer and more intense conscious experience more frequently than the average person.

To be remembered here is that the higher the frequency of energy, the more information it can encode, as per Planck's Law; and that more information as higher Hertz per second results in a richer conscious experience. It therefore seems feasible that the cellular microtubule *lattices of tubulin* (a molecular tubular lattice) could organically form the actual material framework of a *cell's binary-perspective lattices*, where massive gamma-synchronous quanta of Mind, manifesting in Consciousness-intended locations encoded on the perspective lattices, produce a cohesive experience of correlated binary perspectives in the brain. *Once more we are correlating the AQAL Cube lattices, as a cosmological model, with a cell's actual structural lattices of tubulin.*

The question remains, how does Hameroff's proposed "gamma synchrony" actually create those moments of awareness in the brain, like the frames-per-second of a movie?

The author proposes that the AQAL Cube model differentiates the Eight Primordial Perspectives on a fundamental molecular level *as the tubulin lattices* within the cell. *Each* of the 64 reversed-perspective tubulin lattices is encoded to receive its correlated AFP quantum codon, thus experientially activating the intended Fundamental Perspective. In this scenario, the AFP codon as a quantum perspective of Mind is an experiential key that *instantly* identifies its correlated lock in the cell's tubulin perspective lattice through torsional wave entanglement. And once finding that lock, the quantum key turns, resulting in a correlated cellular experience, a quantum moment of Mind-body experience from that perspective intended by the AFP codon – exactly as Hameroff suggests. In this way we completely explain how a Subtle Intention is actually enacted as a correlated Concrete Extension; *thus explaining the Consciousness-Mind-Energy continuum.*

Cerebral neuronal experiential processing, as described above, is slowed down to speeds limited by bioelectric exchanges within the tubulin lattices of the neurons. However, for meditators operating above 80 Hz, their Mind and Consciousness can quantum expand those limits exponentially. Even in Space-time Torsional Waves are not limited by the speed of light, but travel at "infinite" speeds, thereby giving Consciousness an instantaneous "omnipresence", an informational "omniscience", and an immanent "omnipotence".

It would therefore appear that Consciousness is the great Subtle organizing principle that organizes its entry into Concrete existence as Mind through the "play dough" of Zero-Point Field physical energy, or Mind-field; and which it subsequently molds into lower frequency vehicles as physical Life. Seen in this way it could be said that the origin of Life is Consciousness. This is suggestive of a return to a quasi-Lamarckian view of evolution: Consciousness, as the experiencer, first organizes organic intelligence as its primary means of physical experience. That organic intelligence in turn organizes inorganic intelligence as its secondary means of physical experience. Either way, the Subtle Consciousness remains the experiencer and Concrete Energy, both organically intelligent as Mind and inorganically intelligent as Artificial Intelligence, is merely its Concrete experience.

As a result, both the evolutionary debate and the Artificial Intelligence debate regarding physical forms becomes totally one-sided when neglecting how the Consciousness monad "volves" via all those physical forms. For example, the Internet as an AI extension of Mind is fast-tracking our evolution by making information exponentially available to us. This growing inter-connectivity between Consciousness, Mind and Energy moves the Origin of Life and Consciousness debate towards an all-embracing Integral Relativity.

However, new developments in Thermodynamics would at first appear to put all of this in question. In compliance with the Second Law of Thermodynamics, Jeremy England of MIT has formulated the tendency of energy structures to dissipate heat, such as in solar radiation or in deep-sea thermo-volcanic vents, by building self-replicating structures that become more complex the more heat there is to be dissipated. With one formula he laid down the basis of creating the degree of self-organizing organic complexity that hitherto had been attributed to "life" and "life-forms". This indeed blurs the organic distinction between the living and the non-living. From the Abstract of his *arXiv* (2014) paper:

Building on past fundamental results in far-from-equilibrium statistical mechanics, we demonstrate a generalization of the Helmholtz free energy for the finite-time stochastic evolution of driven Newtonian matter. By analyzing this expression term by term, we are able to argue for a general tendency in driven many-particle systems towards self-organization into states formed through exceptionally reliable absorption and dissipation of work energy from the surrounding environment...

Life forms are the most exemplary in being able to reproduce/replicate and dissipate heat. At the level of complexity of the human brain, this structure metabolizes 80% of the body's oxygen. So England's formula is being hailed a jewel in the crown of materialistic science by demonstrating that the origin of life, and therefore consciousness, is thermodynamics.

England's formula makes the claim that the entire Concrete Domain is purely an energetic system where pockets of negentropy, such as in a solar system, can generate the complexity required for physical life, its energetic processes and processing as awareness. In other words, there now seems to be full transparency that Mind/Brain and AI/Computer are mere organic and inorganic equivalents as Concrete Energy processors, and that once AI goes organic they will be one, as in Ray Kurtzweil's (2005) *The Singularity Is Near*. However, when we define Mind as the *experiential* processing of the full Concrete Spectrum, it is easy to overlook the subtle implication – then Who/What is the *Experiencer*? The added implication is that there is no longer an onus for a physical Experiencer of what is being physically experienced as Mind. And England's formula cannot solve that.

On the other hand, Quantum Field Theory *does* place an onus on a non-physical Consciousness. Its central thesis is that a conscious observer collapses a wave function to a particle/torsional vortex with mass. Quantum Mechanics defined an observer as either a device or the operator of a device, meaning that a conscious observer may or may not be key to a wave collapse. However, as QM evolved into Quantum Consciousness, non-physical Consciousness became more of a player, with complications, such as: did the universe exist before life appeared to observe it? It did. It didn't. It did *and* it didn't depending on the choice you make. But from the very outset, the founders of Quantum Mechanics favored the consciousness of the observer as being responsible. Max Planck, John Wheeler and Werner Heisenberg all saw a quantum link between human awareness and the Divine as co-creators. From the Internet, an un-sourced quote of Max Planck says:

I regard consciousness as fundamental. I regard matter as a derivative from consciousness. We cannot get behind consciousness. Everything that we talk about, everything that we regard as existing, postulates consciousness... There is no matter as such. All matter originates and exists only by virtue of a force. We must assume behind this force is the existence of a conscious and intelligent Mind. This Mind is the matrix of all matter.

One hundred years later it seems things are coming full circle back to that realization.

If it does take a conscious observer to collapse an intangible wave into a tangible particle, or an intangible torsional wave into a tangible standing "wavicle", then we can extend that hypothesis as a macrocosmic process of Kosmic unfolding: Kosmogenesis begins with the Primal Polarity of a Primordial Subject taking a Primordial Objective Perspective, thus collapsing its Primordial Wave Function into a Primordial Matrix. Perhaps that is what Planck, Wheeler and Heisenberg were intuiting. Implied is that the quantum effect of a conscious observer provides an analogical basis of "proof" of the origin of the Universe, simply as an observed effect of the One Knower. We examine this next.

Chapter Twelwe

INTEGRAL RELATIVITY AND THE PRIMARY AXIS INJUNCTION

THROUGHOUT THE BROAD spectrum of this book we have explored the perspectival Integral Relativity between Consciousness, Mind and Energy. When the Spectrum of Consciousness is viewed in parallel with the Spectrum of Energy, our evolution through the Spectrum of Consciousness leads us to Who we are, and our evolution through the Spectrum of Energy leads us to What we are.

Energy, or *En-ergia*, means "at work"; which implies that Energy can be correctly defined as the activity of a doer. If Subtle Consciousness is the doer through Intent, and Energy is the doing through Extent, then Mind is the Concrete experience of Subtle Consciousness "at work" as Energy. When Consciousness is *en-quietus*, "at rest", implied is that there is no Mind, no Energy, only the Experiencer. This is the basis of perspectival Integral Relativity.

Laszlo (2014) continues in *"The Primacy of Consciousness"*:

Our whole experience is a construction in the mind, a form appearing in consciousness. These mental forms are composed not of physical substance but of "mindstuff". We imagine that the world out there is like the forms that appear in consciousness, but it turns out, that in nearly every aspect, the external is not at all like the images created in the mind. What appear to us as fundamental dimensions and attributes of the physical world—space, time, matter and energy are but the fundamental dimensions and attributes of the forms appearing in consciousness.

In the chapter differentiating Mind and Consciousness, as a perceptive relativity between Knower, Means of Knowing and Known, it became apparent that Consciousness, the Consciousness monad or Soul, is simply the experiential projection of the Causal Witness into full-spectrum Subtle reality. Similarly, Mind is simply the experiential projection of the Subtle Consciousness into full-spectrum Concrete reality. This is downward causation, where the Knower through experiential Knowledge assumes form. In terms of the Consciousness monad, or Soul, this is the imperative to incarnate and get involved in Concrete experience. Upward causation is the reverse, where the Knower through experiential Knowledge resumes formlessness. Again, for the Soul, this is the imperative to evolve towards Enlightenment

Experiential Knowledge, or Mind, is therefore a two-way mirror connecting the Knower to the Known, where downward causation is the pursuit of experiential Knowledge of the Known and upward causation is the pursuit of experiential Knowledge of the Knower. This was the famous injunction of Socrates – "Know thy Self", meaning have the Supreme Knowledge of the Supreme Knower.

Amrit Sorli is one of the few scientists making the differentiation between Consciousness and Mind. In *New Horizons of Relativity Theory* (2013) he says:

A conscious observer is a reference system at absolute rest. In the realm of physics, the observer is an integral part of the experiment. Speaking out of personal experience and the personal experiences of many other people who practice meditation, I can add that consciousness has the function of observation. Truly, in essence the observer is consciousness itself. The same consciousness is watching the world through the vehicle of the senses of individual men. Most people are experiencing the world tied and bound-up within the limited field of their minds. Conscious-

ness, on the other hand, works only as an observer that cannot see its own origin. When you awaken into true consciousness, you recognize that the "observer" is a pure function of consciousness...

With the beginning of the subjective exploration of consciousness, physics will start to use consciousness as a research tool for discerning the adequacy of scientific models within the world...

For the conscious observer, changes happen in the "eternal now", or as Albert Einstein put it: NOW. A conscious observer is present in each point of space. When our body moves, the conscious observer remains the still point. A conscious observer is the only reference system in the universe that does not move and does not change, it is in absolute rest. This realization gives added dimension and elegance to the Theory of Relativity. The starting point of physics and its research is over time becoming one involving the observer/consciousness. He observes the universe, he supervises mind which builds models of the world; he examines the adequacy of models with physical world.

*The observer/consciousness is the same in each physicist and is giving physics another level of objectivity and a chance to be a truly "objective science", which exists independently of the human mind. **"Subjective experience" is tinged with personality, thoughts and emotions of the person's mind, whereas, "objective experience" is the experience of consciousness itself, which is independent of the mind** [author's bold]. Restated another way, "objective" is what we experience when we are grounded in the awareness of the conscious observer.*

In other words, Existence through all its Domains is a holarchy of AQAL Witness perspectives. For example, we have seen on the AQAL Cube psychograph (Figure 22) how an individual's awareness can occupy different Levels for different Octant/Lines. But because each individual as a Knower identifies generally around a Level average on the Spectrum of Consciousness, any "reality" being witnessed is an interpretation relative to that Level of Consciousness. An illusion is therefore an "apparent reality" when it has no transparency on that Level of Consciousness, where the greater reality behind it cannot be seen until evolving to a higher Level.

Wherever our Witness is located on any Octant/Line of the Consciousness Spectrum, that is the Level of reality we identify with from that Octant perspective. The relativity between Consciousness and Energy is therefore Level specific throughout the Consciousness/Energy Spectrums. This is again supported by Heisenberg's Uncertainty Principle, which demonstrates how subject and object, as observer and observed, are mutually inclusive as a perspective-induced illusion; and that in the relative realms of manifestation, nothing is certain. The inference here is that only the undifferentiated One Knower is the One Certainty, the One Reality.

There is a conceptual danger here of throwing the Kosmic baby out with the bathwater when we judge that baby as a dualistic "illusion", as ultimately not real, and therefore to be "shunned" by the spiritual aspirant. However, this entire Kosmos (as kosmogenesis) is the result of duality-formations, as a series of polarity differentiations of that One Energy. In other words, that One Energy is still at the core of every form it takes, and every form therefore has inherent reality. This is the meaning of "form is formless, and formless is form". So the Kosmos assumes its full meaning when we can *re-member* (as reverse kosmogenesis) all those dualities as polarities, all the way back to our Primal Polarity as Consciousness and Energy; from where we can then enjoy the entire Creation in that non-dual realization. Non-dual Bliss is the experience of being able to perceive the innate "radiant glow" of the formless within each form.

The Chinese Tree of Life cosmogram in Figure 7 shows how those polarities branch out like a tree in kosmogenesis. We return to that model shown here in tabular form in Figure 33.

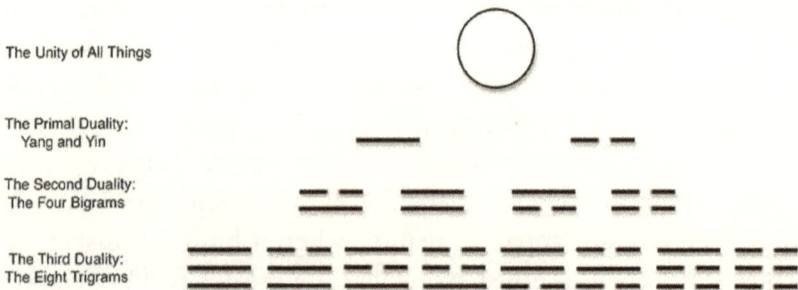

Figure 33. The Chinese Tree Of Polarity Formations

All subject/object dualities emerge from the One Knower, as a result of the Primordial Subject (Yang), taking a Primordial Objective Perspective (Yin). As a quantum analogy we could say that in the beginning, the Primordial Subject, in taking a Primordial Objective Perspective, collapsed its Primordial Wave Function into the Primordial Matrix. Applying this same paradigm through the process of Kosmic unfolding gives an Integral map of the Kosmos of three initial levels of subject/object polarity, and on through the entire Subtle and Concrete spectrums of manifestation. In the end, on planet Earth, a conscious observer collapses a wave of Consciousness by Intent, and experiences a correlated moment of Mind extending that Intent into bodily effect. Figure 34 shows the kosmogenesis of subject-object polarities.

The Primordial One Knower
Non-Dual Domain

Meta-Causal Domain

1. Supreme Knower   2. Supreme Knowledge
Subject as Kosmic Patrix   Object as Kosmic Matrix

Causal   Domain

1. Causal Consciousness	2. Causal Energy	3.Causal Mind	4. Causal Matrix
Subject as Experiencer	Object as Intention	Subjective Experience	Objective Extension

Subtle   Domain   **Concrete   Domain**

Four Subtle Quadrants 1, 3, 5, 7   Four Concrete Quadrants 2, 4, 6. 8

Fifth Person AQAL Cube

Fourth Person AQAL Cube

Third Person AQAL Cube

Second Person AQAL Cube

First Person AQAL Cube

Figure 34. Kosmic Unfolding as Orders of Polarity Differentiation:

In the Metacausal Domain, or first stage of polarity differentiation, the Kosmic Patrix (*Yang*) and Matrix (*Yin*) are Primordial Consciousness (*Shiva*) and Primordial Energy (*Shakti*) respectively. In the Causal Domain, or second stage of polarity differentiation, the I Ching's First Son, First Daughter, Second Son and Second Daughter are *Consciousness, Energy, Mind* and *Matter,* respectively.

The *Consciousness and Energy Fields* are the polarity precursors of the *Subtle Domain*; and the *Mind and Matter Fields* are the polarity precursors of the *Concrete Domain*. In Causal Level meditation, Consciousness pertains to the Inner Light; Energy pertains to the Inner Music; Mind pertains to Spirit-as-Movement (OM); and Matter pertains to Spirit-as-Matrix (Prana/Soma).

In the same way as the Kosmic Patrix and Matrix are *Subject-Object co-emergents* from the One Knower, so the Subtle and Concrete Domains are *Subject-Object co-emergents* from the Causal Domain. These All-Level co-emergent polarities clearly demonstrate how kosmic unfolding is through both vertical Domain *and* horizontal Level holarchies.

From the Causal Domain, the third stage of polarity differentiation results in the Eight Fundamental Perspectives, which arise from the recombinant organization of Consciousness and Energy at the Subtle pole, and of Mind and Matter at the Concrete pole. *These are the eight "archangelic" creative forces* of most religious cosmologies, and also the 6th Person AQAL Cube. In the Sixth Person, we are looking through Violet Awareness, Bodies and Realms, shown in Figure 35.

Octant 1: Illumined Consciousness. **Octant 2:** Illumined Mind. **Octant 3:** Akashic exchange. **Octant 4:** Pranic exchange. **Octant 5:** Akashic archetypes. **Octant 6:** Quantum Field and Physical Microstructure. **Octant 7:** Akashic Realms. **Octant 8:** Zero Point Field and Physical Macrostructure.

The fourth level of duality, or polarity differentiation, produces 64 permutations of manifestation where each of the above Octants yields eight further recombinant polarity permutations.

To take *Octant 6* as an example, which is the *Quantum Field* from which emerges Subatomic Microstructure, the eight permutations are the Eight "Superstrings" or toroidal vortices that form the vibra-

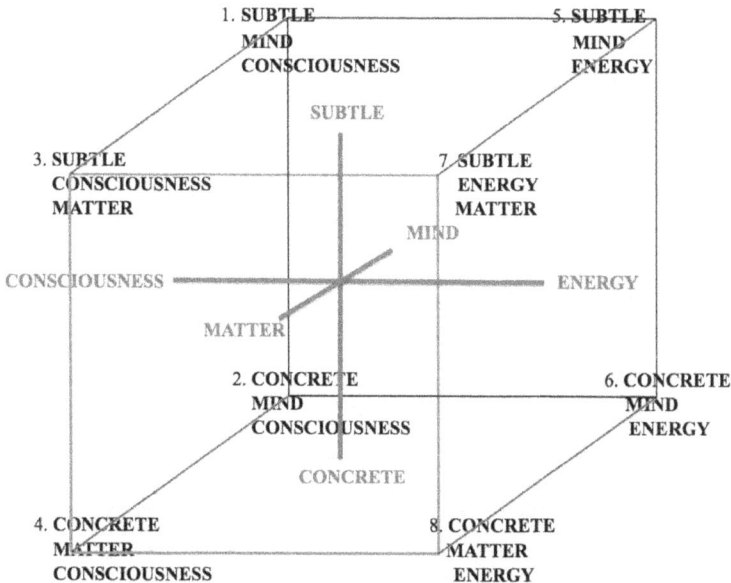

Figure 35. The Causal Eight Fundamental Perspectives

tional templates of all physical matter. Again, they manifest as an Octet of paired polarities, four of which are Forces or energetic action potentials, and four are fundamental particles (better described as standing torsional waves) through which the Forces act. The First Generation of Four Quantum Particles consists of one Quark pair as Up and Down, and one Lepton pair as Electron and Electron Neutrino, shown in Figure 36.

The Four Force Carriers interact with the Four Fundamental Particles as Octets through three stages or "generations" that give birth to the fundamental components of Physical Matter. When we go to the fifth level of duality and beyond on Octant 6, we go into further octaves that comprise the eight atomic electron shells and the entire order of elements on the Periodic Table. In other words, the Eight Fundamental Perspectives, as orders of duality on Octant 6, continue on down as layers of increasing complexity and density into Concrete manifestation.

This same octo-dynamic also applies to the other seven Octants in Figure 35. The other seven Octants of Kosmic manifestation have

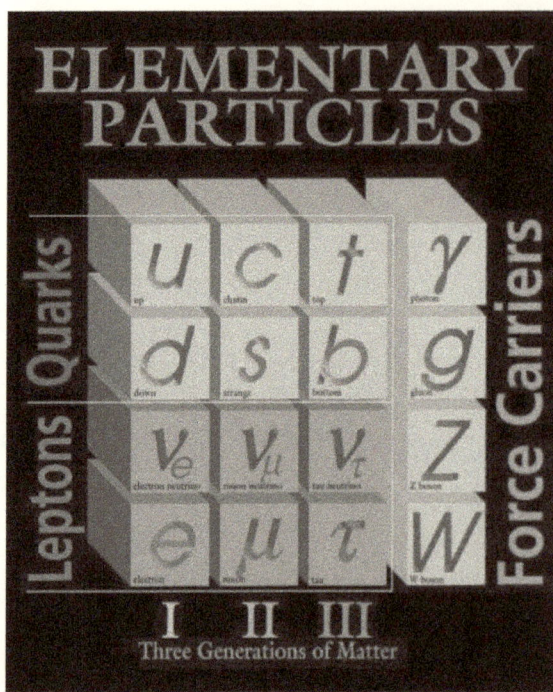

Figure 36. The Standard Model of Fundamental Particles and Forces

been catalogued in various religious cosmologies, the most detailed of which is the Vedantic system of ancient India. Here on Octants 5 and 7 we venture into Subtle Bodies and correlated Realms of Existence called Lokas, which lead us deep into the speculative swamps of unsubstantiated Metaphysics. Suffice it to say here that the Primordial AQAL Cube model in Figure 35 does at least provide for them! For example, I suggest that Wilber's classification of "subtle energies" gets re-evaluated via the differentiation of Octant 5 (Subtle Energy and Subtle Bodies) and Octant 6 (Concrete Quantum and Pranic Energy).

Because duality-as-polarity first emerges in the Meta-Causal, then so does all the ensuing perspectival Integral Relativity generated by the Knower, the Means of Knowing and the Known. Proposed here are the *Three Tenets of Integral Relativity*.

The First Tenet of Integral Relativity is a transcendent but inclusive interpretation of General Relativity - that Energy and Mass are inter-relatable. Extending that through the Primary Axis injunction that differentiates Consciousness, Energy, Mind and Mass:

The First Tenet of Integral Relativity is "The Equation Of Energy With Consciousness", which states: "The Knower taking Subtle perspectives is Consciousness, and Consciousness acting through those perspectives is Energy; where full-spectrum Subtle Consciousness acts through Intent as full-spectrum Subtle and Concrete Energy".

In other words, Full-Spectrum Consciousness at work is Full-Spectrum Energy, whether Local or Non-local. The Energy Spectrum is therefore the matrix, the vehicle, of the Consciousness Spectrum, as per Integral Theory. However, "the vehicle" here includes not only the Subtle vehicles of Consciousness but also the Concrete vehicles of Mind and Body, where full-spectrum Concrete Mind acts, in Extent of that Intent, through full-spectrum Concrete Matter." Car and driver on all Levels.

The Second Tenet of Integral Relativity is a transcendent but inclusive interpretation of the Law of Conservation of Energy - that Energy cannot be created nor destroyed, but only transformed from one state to another. Through the First Tenet equating Energy with Consciousness:

The Second Tenet of Integral Relativity is "The Law of Conservation of Consciousness", which states: "Consciousness cannot be created nor destroyed, but only transformed from one state to another."

In other words, the Consciousness-Energy continuum is all pervasive - infinite and eternal. In this light, the Equation Of Energy With Consciousness and the Law of Conservation of Consciousness essentially become spiritual laws in bearing out Gautama Buddha's assertion in the Pali Canon of the continuity of Consciousness between incarnations. This implies that we even intend our incarnations in an on-going imperative to return to the Source, to the One Knower.

The first two tenets bring us to the final element of the Integral Relativity equation. In General Relativity physical light is Einstein's

Universal Constant in Locality. As an extension of General Relativity, the Non-local Kosmic Constant of Integral Relativity is the Kosmic Light, as the One Knower. If Subtle Consciousness is the "heads" side of the coin and Concrete Mind is the "tails", then the coin itself is the Kosmic Constant, the One Knower. As such, the Knower would be the true Unifier, the Carrier Wave of all superimposed modulations of Consciousness, Mind and Energy. Without any Intent there is only the Carrier Wave, the "Primordial Vibration", the "OM", which is Pure Consciousness, or No-Mind, *En-Quietus*.

So the Third Tenet of Integral Relativity is a transcendent and inclusive interpretation of General Relativity and Heisenberg's Uncertainty Principle, where the very act of observing an energetic phenomenon causes a quantitative and qualitative indeterminacy, the outcome of which nevertheless *conforms to the direct proportionality of its information to its frequency,* as per Planck's constant.

Given that the infinite Primordial Frequency of undifferentiated Energy embraces the totality of experiential information as per Planck's Law:

The Third Tenet of Integral Relativity is "The Law of Kosmic Constancy", which states: "The Kosmic Constant, through which all subsequent phenomena can be experienced as Supreme Knowledge, is the Primordial Frequency of Energy; and via the First and Second Tenets, that Constant is therefore the Supreme Knower".

This sheds new light on the iconic biblical words of John the Divine: "In the Beginning was the Word, and the Word was with God, and the Word was God". This can now be rephrased as: "In the Beginning was the Knowledge, and the Knowledge was with the Knower, and the Knowledge was the Knower". In other words, from such a perspective, the *non-differentiated Pure Consciousness* Subject as the infinite eternal *Supreme Knower,* and the *undifferentiated Pure Energy* Object as the infinite eternal *Supreme Knowledge,* are *not-two.* When Socrates said "Know Your Self", he was saying "Know the Knower".

The cutting-edge mathematician Michael Hockney makes a similar deduction regarding the number Zero, which he proves is both Zero *and* Infinity. It is a mathematical version of Planck's Law, where a primordial "zero" frequency contains "infinite" information. In his book *The Mathematical Universe* Hockney (2014) says:

> What is "nothing"? It's categorically **not** "non-existence". Nothing is actually something. Something is mathematically structured nothingness. The generalized Euler Formula is exactly the miraculous mathematical instrument that allows nothing to be structured...
>
> In order for zero to be the inevitable and inescapable net result of the combination of infinite numbers, all of the numbers must conform with the most powerful analytic formula in the whole of mathematics – Euler's Formula, the great jewel of mathematics: $e^{ix} = \cos x + i \sin x$...
>
> What's so remarkable about Euler's Formula is that it produces perfect balance between negative and positive numbers, between real and imaginary numbers and between zero and infinity. No element is privileged over any other. The net ontological effect of the formula is zero (since the circle's negative half perfectly cancels its positive half), yet this is an "infinite" zero, a structured "nothing" that goes on forever!
>
> In order to include all possible ontological numbers, it's necessary to introduce a more generalized form of Euler's Formula:
>
> $A\, e^{\,i(fx + ö)} = A \cos (fx + ö) + i\, A \sin (fx + ö)$
>
> where A is amplitude, f is frequency and ö = the phase angle (phase shift). In the frequency domain, the three elements necessary to specify a wave are amplitude, frequency and phase, so this generalized formula allows all possible waves to be accommodated.

In other words, even the infinite information encoded in the Primordial Frequency is still according to Amplitude, Frequency and Phase – *the AFP codon!* Where Hockney falls short is in confining conscious awareness to the Concrete Domain (as Mind). However, in our applying the First and Second Tenets of Integral Relativity we can now equate his dimensionless mathematical domain with Consciousness, his Zero with the Supreme Knower, and his Infinity with the Supreme Knowledge. In the same way as he describes Zero/Infinity as two sides of the same coin, so we have described the Supreme Knower (Consciousness) and the Supreme Knowledge (Energy).

The One Knower, as the coin itself, is the culmination of all previous Levels of Epistemic and Ontic AQAL world views, of all knower-to-known polarities – such as Patrix to Matrix, Subject to Object, First Person to Third Person, Subtle Consciousness to Concrete Life, Real Self to Actual Self – where an evolving AQAL worldview elevates the *assumed* Knower up a mountain of mistaken identities, from Mind/Ego to Consciousness/Soul, before reaching the Supreme Witness at the "top".

Most philosophies are altitude-based perspectives, meaning that they are all correct in the context of their altitude and perspective. For example, Idealism is a Third Tier view where beyond all the polarity/duality the Supreme Subject is the only reality. Panpsychism is a Second Tier view, where subjects create their reality objects. Materialism is a First Tier view, where the object is the only reality. Most philosophical debate regarding our ontological being and etymological knowing is really cross-purpose argument coming from *unspecified* levels and perspectives. "Reality", as a philosophical view from a *specified* level and perspective, is true to that level and perspective. Change level, change perspective, change view, change philosophical interpretation.

Furthering that, a Second Tier Consciousness monad (a *Wilber-Newtonian* Blue to Indigo Climber) appreciates the view from half way up the mountain of Cognitive structures. But the Integral Relativity here is whether the Climber is ascending *to* the top or descending *from* the top, giving two completely different worldviews from that altitude. For a returning Third Tier climber, First Tier reality is a non-dual take of being in this world of form in formlessness. This is the Primary Axis volutionary dynamic, where the more our Life-as-experience gets evolved in Consciousness, the more our Consciousness-as-Knower gets experientially involved in our Life. Our volution is therefore an exponential process.

This implies that the Physical Universe is an open, volving, negentropic system, and that it is therefore *not* subject to the entropic, clockwork-like "slowing down" of a closed system. It further implies that there was no Big Bang, nor will there be a "Big Crunch", but more likely that this Concrete Domain is in energetic balance with the Subtle Domain. In that regard, the Three Tenets of Integral Relativity pose a Consciousness/Mind/Energy continuum, and if that proves to be the case, it also proves that the Concrete Domain is an open, negentropic system.

In Nassim Haramein's iconic paper (2013) "Quantum Gravity and the Holographic Mass" he proves that this universe is an open holographic feedback system of energy and information that has the effect of expanding the Physical Universe: On the one hand nonlocal information, which we have called Consciousness, is pouring into locality, and in-forming locality as Mind. On the other hand, as the universe expands, quantum energy is drawn into the mini black hole at the core of *every proton in the universe*, accounting for gravity. But it also accounts for the state of resonant flux of information between the Subtle and Concrete Domains. In other words, Life, as embedded and embodied Consciousness, exemplifies this entire process in its relentless pursuit of its own transcendent Truth.

Chapter Thirteen

TO KNOW THE KNOWER

O UR QUEST FOR identity leads to our asking many *questions*, as a process of orientation and navigation, which irrevocably leads to One Answer. Each Face of Spirit comes with its own fundamental question, which perpetually needs answering to redefine our ever-evolving state of being, shown in Figure 37.

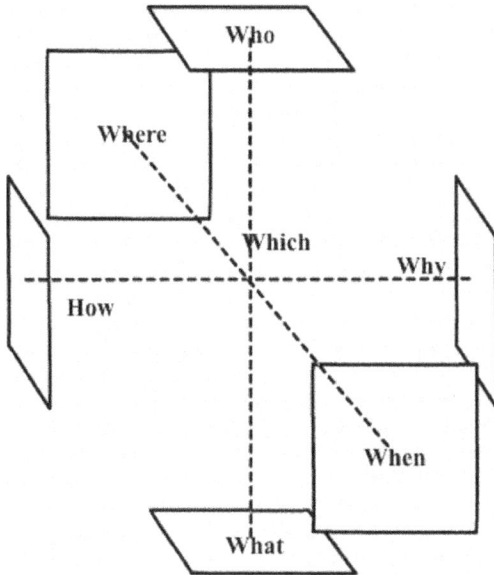

Figure 37. The Six Questions as Polarities

If we are a detective and our quest is to find a murderer, we ask the fundamental questions: **Who** is the victim? **What** happened? **When** and **Where** did it happen? **How** did it happen, and the motive

– **Why?** In the middle is the one person who has the Answer – the perpetrator/Witness. If these questions are now applied to find our own Self, we have: 1. Who am I? 2. What am I doing? 3. Why am I here? 4. How can I know? 5. Where am I going? 6. When will I get there? 7.*Which* Answer we get is about the choices we make to find that Answer. In other words, at the heart of the matter are which choices we make - that either take us towards or lead us away from our Self-knowing.

Our Where and When, as space-time coordinates, plot our intended **Direction** from moment-to-moment in the here/now. Our direction on the road of Life is determined by where we choose on our quest for our individual truth, our purpose, which in time brings us back to loving family and friends with whatever fruits of our journey. Our How and Why are the parameters within which we maintain our **Balance** on our journey. On the one hand, how we choose to use our personal power to the good in sowing the seeds of our actions leads, on the other hand, to the wisdom of why we reap what we sow. Lastly we discover Who and What we are, in choosing to know our Self in whatever Life we live, which is our **Growth**. As our cycles of growth take us towards spiritual knowing, our material being unfolds in its beauty.

Often it seems that on our road of life we had "no choice" but to end up where we do. This is the result of the *unconscious* choices we make as we go along. But our *conscious* evolution is in making conscious choices to engage in transformative action. And our transformation is both inner *and* outer. Inner realization comes along with realizing we can make a difference out there. As we evolve, our evolutionary imperative transforms to our Enlightenment imperative, at which point we start asking the right questions about our choices.

All this questioning brings us to the One Answer that was waiting to be discovered in the midst of it all. The Ancient Traditions are very clear about that One Answer, but not so clear as to where to find it. Rarely do they say that the Answer has been under our very nose all along – in our very breath. Rarely do they say that from our awareness of breath (*Spira*) comes our awareness of Spirit (*Spiritus*).

In our breath cycle is hidden our potential for greater Consciousness, a potential that escalates exponentially the more we become breath-aware. The moment our attention on our breath lapses, then the potential in that particular breath is aborted, but when our attention becomes constant our potential can become realized. When our breath cycle is raised from an unconscious respiratory act, operated by the *sympathetic nervous system*, to a fully conscious conspiratory act, operated by the *central nervous system* of our spinal chord, then our consciousness of breath leads to Breath consciousness in our spinal chord, which transforms our awareness. The central canal in our spinal chord leads directly into the brain and its cavities, where our inner experience of the Breath beyond the breath has its physical roots to flower.

A simple mechanical awareness of our breath cycle does not lead to higher awareness, because an aspiring sincere receptivity is needed to form a relationship with Spirit in a state of Grace with the Consciousness we aspire to. In this way our humble breath awareness becomes as a prayer, an affirmation that our awareness may expand into that of Spirit.

Since ancient times an Enlightened teacher has been considered essential for the aspirant's ascent into Spirit. Even the most determined of spiritual practitioners become entrenched as their awareness evolves from Ego to Soul, when the awareness becomes spiritual Ego instead of Soul, and when negative emotions find new forms of self-righteous expression. This is where Grace and guidance are sorely needed. Just as someone who is drowning is in need of a swimmer to come to the rescue, so those who are bogged down on the spiritual path need guidance from someone who knows the way.

A manual written by an anonymous 7th century Taoist master for his pupils, called *The Secret of the Golden Flower*, makes it very clear that those who wish to know *The Secret of the Golden Flower* need the guidance of the one who already knows It's Secret. The manual describes beautifully how the Seed that becomes the Golden Flower is watered with the Breath. There the teacher says: *"The great Tao comes forth from the center. Do not seek the primordial Seed outside! The Seed that becomes the Golden Flower!"*

Our true nature from which we emerged, and to which we re-merge, is that Seed of Consciousness. As an undifferentiated Seed it contains the entire vast potential of Creation, like the so-called Primal Atom before the Big Bang. And just as in the cycles of nature, where a seed returns to a seed via its flowers and fruits, so through endless cycles the growth of awareness starts from and returns to an infinitesimality containing all, like an acorn contains an oak tree.

The true extent of the infinitesimal, as a seed within a seed within a seed, embraces all the realms of awareness that one book described as the many Mansions in the House of God. Ultimately we realize the Seed is our true Self: our awareness *of* God as Divine Knowledge, and our awareness *as* God as the One Knower. Every religion has a word for it, a symbol for it: The Pearl of Great Price, the Jewel in the Heart of the Lotus, the Grain of Mustard Seed, the World Egg, the Philosopher's stone.

The Seed is also a symbol on many levels of experience. The cycle of a seed through the course of a year can be a metaphor for our own life cycle: Our being takes root in this earthly life, attains stature, buds, flowers and comes to fruition. If we are a seed of awareness when we are cast into incarnation, sown into this field of dreams, what flower, what fruit may we yield? "As we sow, so do we reap" say the Ancient Traditions. In the arena of this physical universe, our awareness and our actions are inter-related, inter-dependent. In this sense, the seed may be interpreted as any action by which the fruits or repercussions or consequences will be inevitably reaped, for better or worse.

The seed of any personal action is rooted in our own compost of inertia, desire and fear. Inertia denies us that one act that would have been our redemption. Desire binds us to our small sense of self, more so when selfish, less so when dedicated to a greater good, and even less when we act out of love. We are bound by our actions least of all when our life is an act of love for the Creator. At that point, our greater sense of self, our spiritual love, is interfacing and identifying with "The Seed that becomes the Golden Flower", Enlightenment, Universal Consciousness. Fear denies us the courage to open the door of our dark, safe closet to the blinding Beauty that we really are.

But when our inertia, desire and fear are completely composted, it becomes clear that we are each a Garden in which our Seed of divine potential can be cultivated, where the Gardener is the Creator's guidance needed for our growth, in whatever form it may come.

It has also been said that the true temple of God is the human body ("the Kingdom of Heaven is within"). So Jesus clearing the moneychangers out of the temple is a timeless metaphor of abusing our temple when using it solely for sensory satisfaction. Our moneychangers are our worldly desires, which we would never throw out unless we cultivate a desire to know our transcendent nature. The process of clearing the temple, preparing the garden, making a sanctified space wherein the Creator's presence can be experienced is a gradual, deliberate work that is both inside and outside.

Simple preparations in bodily purification are pure, fresh foods; pure water to drink; moderation in meat, alcohol and sex; breath awareness; resulting in *detachment from libidinous drives and a body-identity.*

Simple preparations in mental purification are the practices of non-violence, truthfulness and self awareness as breath, releasing overactive/reactive emotions and thought processes into the breath, resulting in *calmness and detachment from body-mind identity.*

Simple preparations for our *detachment from our limited, self-serving ego-identity* is in turning our concerns towards the welfare of others, including that of other creatures. This opens our heart in compassion and releases us from killing others for food or gain, or from taking advantage in any way. To create change we do not need to become embroiled in political strife and activism. We need only to become exemplary in our own life. Leading by example transforms passive resistance to active assistance, where we find our own way to make a difference for those around us. For example, when one considers there is more food waste than hungry mouths it can feed, simple arrangements with local restaurants and food markets can divert waste food from a dumpster to a dinner.

Simple preparations in cultivating our spiritual awareness are to indulge our self in spiritually inspiring company, and to open our heart to the Divine. This results in *detachment from worldly identification, stress and strife* that we may move and be moved towards the recognition of the Divine within our self. Buddha's fifth Dharma on the Eightfold Path, Right Livelihood, is about our becoming an instrument of the Divine-as-Creator. Joe Campbell called it "follow your bliss". Apparently, misinterpreting this advice led many into hedonistic debaucheries; but taking "Bliss" in its elevated meaning we are talking about the experience of being moved by, or being an instrument of, Divine Inspiration. "Right Livelihood" implies that we are each endowed with a meaningful creative skill, a talent special to us that can be used to inspire those around us. And part of finding our truth is in discovering our unique creativity that brings us joy. We do not have to become an Olympic athlete or Julliard pianist to accomplish this. Even to become a consummate parent providing a loving home for a loving child may be our path to joy in a meaningful life. Whatever it is, when we do find our bliss we become a beacon of inspiration to others in our life. And yet, living our bliss is not really through some objective out there, it is about simply being in bliss-consciousness, which *is* our Truth, our *Sat Chit Anand*.

Buddha's Eightfold Path was a means of organizing our daily routine into a path of transformation embracing all of our Individual, Interior, Collective and Exterior life. Integral Theory calls this "Integral Life Practice". The author's introduction to what Integral Theory would later call "Integral Life Practice" (ILP) was in 1972, when he met his Master Prem Rawat at his home by the Upper Ganges in the Himalayan foothills. His home was also an ashram ("shelter") housing a number of followers. Immediately apparent was the utter tranquility and ease in which the entire place functioned under the kind watchfulness of the elder Mahatmas. The daily routine was an ancient Hindu classic version of ILP: Meditation, *Satsang* ("company of Truth") and Service; or the "I", "We" and "It" as First, Second and Third Person practices.

Later, Prem dissolved the ashram system, and now calls meditation Practice, *satsang* Listening and service Participation. In our Participation in selfless action we discover our Goodness. In Listening to the wisdom of the enlightened we discover our Truth. In the Practice of being our inner peace we discover our Beauty. The meditation Practice aspect, a form of Raja Yoga techniques that Prem calls Knowledge, is a very ancient one based on the inversion of the senses to experience inner Light, inner Music, inner Breath-sense and inner Taste.

So this entire three-fold process is the means of cultivating the soil of our soul, the process of removing the rocks in our stony ground so that the Seed of divine awareness may be planted in us, and may flourish in us, and may later bear the fruit of Enlightenment. This is by true meditation.

The meditation process is twofold. Because our sense of identity is conditioned by the way we use our Mind, then the first part of the process is to clarify our Mind by becoming *objectively self-aware*: observing the way we live and behave through each thought, word and deed. We are then able to consciously eliminate the turbulence, the emotions and psychoses and resulting behaviors, which go against our clarity and peace of mind. The second part is internal, where we cultivate focused subjective self-awareness through our *attention on each breath* we take. This leads to a level of inner vigilance in which we lose our attachment to our lesser identities, as our Mind becomes transparent to the true Consciousness behind it.

We have seen how our human form is a model for the Kosmos, only this time we focus specifically on/in the human head. Some great Sage described our head as the Square Foot Field containing a Square Inch House. A cubic foot temple containing a cubic inch altar would be more appropriate. The three axes of our head extend between the eyes (Direction), between the ears (Balance) and our vertical axis to the parietal foramen at the crown of our head (Growth). They intersect exactly in the pineal gland, which is the center of our Attention/Second Attention/ Witness. This is where we witness our superposition as the Knower of Pure Consciousness.

When we have received the Grace to enter deep meditation – the type that Buddha guided his followers into what he called Perfect Absorption – we center on the pineal gland at the intersection of the three axes: We will begin to see the inner Light of Consciousness, hear the inner Music of pure Energy, and breathe the inner Spirit Breath into the brain's ventricles surrounding the pineal. Deep meditation is the fine-tuning of our Attention-as-Witness towards pure Energy at the "Ultra-violet" end where its amplitude, frequency and polarity become Emptiness, Silence and Stillness. This is where pure Energy, unrealized as Unconsciousness, is realized as pure Consciousness in an imploding experience called Enlightenment. Our duality, when our Mind is unconscious of the pure Energy upholding the entire Kosmos, is resolved in its conscious merging with that pure Energy as Universal Consciousness. Our Eight Fundamental Perspectives expand through the Spectrum as a shimmering spectral bubble of awareness from its center of pure Energy-as-Unconsciousness towards Pure Energy realized as Pure Consciousness. Finally our bubble, the membrane within which is our domain of dual awareness, pops or implodes in a non-dual experience called Enlightenment.

From the non-dual "Ultra-Violet" perspective of the One Knower, the entire Kosmos is merely a Super-Mind experience. As such the Kosmos is merely another disposable Consciousness-and-Life structure, just like the human Mind-and-Body. The universal law that anything created faces destruction applies to the entire Kosmos, to the spectrum of Consciousness and Life, to gods and gollums alike. Only the primordial One Knower remains. And for us, it remains to know the One Knower.

On that note we come to the conclusion of this book. As its title suggests, "Knowing the Knower" is a scientific approach to knowing and understanding our unfathomable Self through the burgeoning fields of New Science. In its present state, the bulk of the scientific community is still beleaguered with a material view of existence, and a view that any non-material investigations by the New (Pseudo) Sciences are irresponsible forays into mysticism and the supernatural, which inevitably lead back to some God-force as explanation. As if Intelligent Design was not enough, now the Aether is back!

For example, the New Biologist Rupert Sheldrake has Morphic Fields to explain how life plays energetically with form outside of genetic constraints. He says that the entire history of science has been a progression into new orders of phenomena, through reversals from what was once considered "supernatural" to become natural, once the new energetics and laws came to be understood. The progress of New Sciences, such as Quantum Cosmology equating non-local energy with Consciousness, is no exception. And even if some God-force does ultimately emerge as a proven scientific explanation, at least it will have nothing to do with religion! And it will be truly natural. In other words, the progression is towards our true nature.

The Noetic Sciences are looking within, to the subjective experiential nature of both individuals and populations. The Human Consciousness Project is finding similar evidence as Sheldrake, that on some level our awareness is shared by all, and that worldly events ripple through our "common pond" to cause instantaneously shared changes and shifts of perspective. On some level we are discovering that we are all connected consciously and energetically, and that our domain of interconnectivity is expanding more rapidly than the shockwave of a supernova. In other words, Consciousness is also making itself known to us. The Knower and the Known are becoming One, and our evolution is becoming self-evidently Self-Aware.

Scientifically, the main problem in integrating this cross-disciplined trajectory towards a "self-aware Kosmos" is the lack of a meta-model that unifies all this knowledge into a true Theory/Practice of Everything. Quantum Cosmologists and Quantum Physicists are the main toters of "T.O.E's", but their "Everything" happens to be limited to Energy as a Unified Field. Whereas when Consciousness is brought into the equation with Energy, this more inclusive scientific version of "Everything" has few takers.

One such claimant as a T.O.E. that includes Consciousness, Energy, and all the goings-on in the known Physical Domain, including evolution and the history of human consciousness, is Ken Wilber's Integral Theory. But once again his "Everything" model happens to not include the Non-Physical Domain that is rapidly disclosing itself in the Noetic Sciences.

The evidence is overwhelming that Wilber's Integral model, the AQAL Square, conflates the Subtle AQAL dimensions of Consciousness, Bodies and Realms with the Concrete AQAL dimensions of Mind, Bodies and Realms. It also conflates the Eight Personal Pronoun Perspectives *per Person* to a mere four. The Personal Pronouns give our personal awareness the dimensionality we need for the perceptual evaluation of our individual and collective evolution. These conflations have prevented Integral Theory from evolving in the way it should – as a Second Tier model differentiating the Subtle and Concrete Domains through each Person. The AQAL Cube and its resulting tenets of Integral Relativity integrate Consciousness, Mind and Energy with our Knower, Means of Knowing and Known as a continuum of volving perspectives.

Wilber's First Tier AQAL Square model leads to an understanding of our Concrete actuality, of our Life and Mind. The Second Tier AQAL Cube model is a call to wake up to the reality of our Subtle Consciousness, as an all-pervading organizing presence embedded in and embodied by the entire fabric of this Physical Universe. The process of this Universe becoming Self-Aware is through the unfolding of our own Subtle Consciousness monad, or Soul. This is a volutionary process *correlated with* the unfolding of our Concrete Mind. We need to make that conscious correlation to effect our transition, as a global humanity, from First to Second Tier awareness. The culmination of this Integral process is *world Peace* - when *every individual* in every nation has evolved all Octants of Knower and Known all the way to a *Supreme Knower* of a *Supreme Knowledge*.

FIRST, SECOND
AND THIRD PERSON
PERSPECTIVES

I n Excerpt D of his "Kosmos Trilogy", Ken Wilber said that our perceptions are the result of our perspectives taking perspectives, and that even Second and Third Person Perspectives are objects of our First Person as primary subject. In other words, perspectives taking perspectives are binary perspectives, and our perceptions are the result of the binary perspectives between a primary subject and its object.

In First Person, a binary perspective is of our interior awareness. Verbal language is our most explicit exterior means of expressing our interior awareness. Other implicit signals like bodily expressions are secondary to the precise communication that language provides. And yet language itself is a relatively simple construction, made of six main components: Nouns (tangible things), Verbs (actions and processes), Adverbs (modus operandi), Adjectives (descriptive), Prepositions (relational changes) and Pronouns (overall perspectives). In his ITC Conference paper Bruce Alderman (2013) calls them "the Six Views". They are our means of telling our story through our perceptions. All Six Views give the bigger picture of our entire sensory awareness, and it may come as no surprise that the picture is yet another version of the Six Faces of Spirit.

Once again, in asking the Six Questions, we use the correlated Six Views for framing meaningful answers: "Who" and "What" are conveyed by Pronouns and Nouns; "When" and "Where" are conveyed by Prepositions and Conjunctions; "How" is conveyed by Verbs and Adverbs; and "Why" is somewhat the wildcard, where meaning-making emerges from all Six Views. In this book we have favored the Personal Pronouns because they are the primary expression of our self-awareness as our Who and What, our Consciousness and Mind, our Knower and its experiential Knowledge.

Language comes into being as a result of our self-awareness trying to express what we perceive and intend in a meaningful way to others. A consensus of such meaning-making becomes a culture with a shared world-view. Language tends to be used subconsciously and reactively in dealing with all the input our senses receive. In such a scenario language is largely impotent, providing a relational lubricant for validating our individual existence amongst others. But used in full consciousness, language becomes powerful and transformative, like a radiant energy field that commands the attention, inspires and moves – as a true extension of Consciousness. The voice and words of the prophets, bards, literary greats, as well as politicians and tyrants, are a testament to the power of language over time.

It is no secret that the deliberate "dumbing down" of populations by corporate-owned media and corporate-cut education results in nations of almost illiterate "sheeple", who are raised to be the modern slaves. But like the American slaves in the time of Lincoln, "sheeple" still have a voice. Even without education, the yearning and inspiration to be free is no less powerful, and such a voice is no less eloquent. Such a voice on the internet can awaken a world overnight. Not long ago in the Middle East and North Africa, several nations became poised for revolution through their youth communicating and sharing their ideals over the internet. To become a powerful voice in the face of a powerful establishment, or in the heart of a somnambulant crowd, requires a feat of clarity - the kind of clarity that can turn a mob into a meeting.

The more we awaken to consciousness, the more power our Six Views command. As far as powerful language goes, the Six Views are like the six basic colors required for painting a word-picture, and our goal is to become an artist. As we evolve we become more self-aware of what we say, as well as of what we do. In a shadow world, language is reduced to an instrument of deception and lies that can hold entire nations in tyranny and disempowerment. But along with individual consciousness comes individual empowerment, and the power to create change and transformation in the collective consciousness around us.

There is indeed a growing sense of "We-ness" as global crisis looms, and as the connectivity provided by the internet brings isolated individuals closer together. In times past, "We the people" lost patience with the powers that were and overthrew them in bloody revolutions. In this time, with weapons technology, that would be a disaster. In the spirit of Gandhi's non-violence, the "Occupy" movement protesting the greed of Wall Street and its Plutocracy grew overnight into a global phenomenon, as a means of protesting an entire spectrum of disenfranchisement. Despite its powerful altruism, that "We" movement eventually collapsed in a similar fashion to that of the Muslim students protesting fundamentalism, or the "Peace and Love" movement of the Sixties protesting war.

We now look at the possibility that all inter-subjective and inter-objective "We" and "Us" movements have a flawed premise when, as First Person collectives, trying to accomplish Second and Third Person agendas. Even the standard model of Integral Theory uses the "We" identity in a Second Person context. What does this imply?

"We" is actually my own First Person Plural self-take on my having a shareable world view. "Shareable" is the operative word, where my inner inter-subjective awareness "We" is poised to make a Second Person inter-subjective exchange with someone else. Until that happens, there are two individuals in proximity, and *even in communion*, but in First Person awareness. It is only when we *communicate* with each other, or with the "enemy", that the whole ballgame shifts to an "I-You", Second Person reality, and we know the power of our sharing. The "I-You" space is where the ball gets hit out of the park. For "me" to really understand "you", I not only need to know my First Person space, but also your Second Person space, and vice versa.

Integral Theory has not differentiated a First or Second Person AQAL map, and the proposed First and Second Person AQAL Cubes fully differentiate all the nuanced perspectives required for *inter-personal* understanding. The significant implications involve the power to meaningfully communicate as ambassadors, diplomats, leaders, governments, and entire nations of individuals without a voice.

Between the Eight First Person Perspectives alone there are 8 x 8 = 64 binary perspectives we can take of our self-situation. And when "I" bring these to "your" table and consider the 64 ways "I" can now *see* "you", and "you" can *see* "me" back, there are a myriad nuances to be shared. When two poets come together in the name of the muse, the Earth quakes. We need to recognize our personal power to communicate our vision and our greatness, which is that of our own Self. To know "my" Self is to know "You". "You know what I'm saying? You hear me?"

If Integral Theory is to practice a leading role in global transformation, it is vital to expand the Integral model to *octo-dynamic* First and Second Persons. In this way the self's "We" space can expand as a truly shared "I-You-Them" space in full consciousness, where we can enjoy each other's beauty, truth and goodness.

Following are the 24 personal pronoun perspectives through the First, Second and Third Persons.

First Person Pronoun Perspectives

Detailed below are the Eight First Person Perspectives through four representative Levels, which are designated by colors of the Wilber-Newtonian spectrum. Each Perspective includes the corresponding Line(s) in Integral Theory.

Octant 1: *Proximate Self* as the "I" Consciousness. Self-identity witnessing through Levels of assumed identity states. *Lines: Proximate Self-identity, spiritual identity*. Representative Levels of Self-identity-as-witness are: Red – Id identity (Consciousness fused with the Lower Mind); Orange – Ego identity (Consciousness fused with

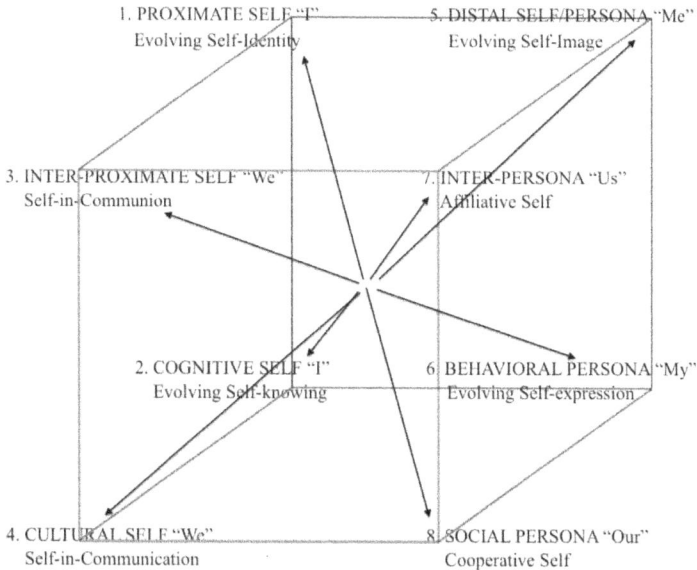

1. PROXIMATE SELF "I"
Evolving Self-Identity

5. DISTAL SELF/PERSONA "Me"
Evolving Self-Image

3. INTER-PROXIMATE SELF "We"
Self-in-Communion

7. INTER-PERSONA "Us"
Affiliative Self

2. COGNITIVE SELF "I"
Evolving Self-knowing

6. BEHAVIORAL PERSONA "My"
Evolving Self-expression

4. CULTURAL SELF "We"
Self-in-Communication

8. SOCIAL PERSONA "Our"
Cooperative Self

First Person AQAL Cube.

the Lower Mind); Blue – Soul identity (Consciousness differentiated from Higher Mind). Violet – Supreme Witness (Causal Consciousness and Causal Mind as Non-dual).

Octant 2: *Cognitive Self* as the "I" Mind. Experiential and access awareness, through Fulcrum Levels of intelligence structures. *Lines: All Intelligences, such as cognitive, affective, psychosexual, aesthetic, spiritual.* Representative Levels of experiential intelligence are: Red – Lower Mind sensing, feeling, emoting; Orange – Lower Mind thinking; Blue – Higher Mind visioning; Violet – Causal Mind wisdom/ Akashic experience/Supermind.

Octant 3: *Inter-Proximate Self* as the "We" Consciousness. Shared self through Levels of assumed identity states. *Line: inter-proximate self.* Representative Levels are: Red – Inter-Id as fused "I-We"; Orange – Inter-Ego; Blue – Inter-Soul; Violet – Non-Dual "We".

Octant 4: *Cultural Self* as the "We" Mind. Interpretive shared or common experience as cultural intelligence. *Lines: moral self, worldview self.* Representative Levels are: Red – Tribal member (fused "I-We"); Orange – cultural independent; Blue – cultural visionary; Violet – spiritual iconoclast.

Octant 5: *Distal Self (Persona)* as the "Me" Consciousness. Objectively differentiated from the Proximate Self of Octant 1, the Persona is self-referential as a Self-image. This is the intentional persona of the Enneagram, the objective evaluator of the Self-system and home of the Self- judging Super-Ego. After death existence or Bardo is a projection of this self-evaluation as our Non-Local All-Level Persona. *Line: intentional persona.* Representative Levels as State-stages are: Red – Id-centered, 4th Bardo; Orange – Ego-centered, 3rd Bardo; Blue – Soul-centered, 2nd Bardo; Violet – Pneumo-centered, 1st Bardo.

Octant 6: *Behavioral Persona (Personality)* as the "My" Mind. Objectively differentiated from the Cognitive Self of Octant 2, the Behavioral Persona is the objective expression of Mind as our Personality and its Enneatypes. *Lines: behavioral personalities as applied to cognitive, affective, psychosexual, aesthetic, spiritual.* Representative Levels as Structure-stages are: Red – magic; Orange – rational; Blue – integral; Violet – spiritually wise.

Octant 7: *Inter-Distal Persona* as the "Us" Consciousness. The Social Self-image is a fused "Me- Us" until socio-centric, after which the Social Identity differentiates. Identification with family, organizations and affiliations. After-death identification with others is through the correlated Non-Local All-Level Social Persona. *Line: interpersonal.* Representative Levels as State-stages are: Red – symbiont; Orange – server-dominator; Blue – integrator; Violet – compassionate.

Octant 8: *Social Personality* as the "Our" Mind. The Social Personality evolving as organized and cooperative behavior and experience of social situations. *Lines: sociocultural, relational, ethical.* Representative Levels as Structure-stages: Red – tribal member; Orange – nationalist; Blue – globalist; Violet – utopian.

Second Person Pronoun Perspectives

Second Person research is in serious need of this expanded model, especially for dysfunctional relationships, families, communities and nations. When dealing with a shared binary perspective between two individuals, the Subject has a First Person Cube psychograph, whose Second Person Object has a perceived Second Person Cube psychograph, and vice versa for the other Subject. The differences between the four resulting psychographs reveal the perceptual obstacles.

Octant 1: Proximate Self in individual relationship as "You/ Thou" Consciousness. Individually identifying with and relating to another implies intimacy. In times gone by "Thou" implied true identity, trust and respect reserved for an honored relationship. Representative State-stages are: Red – Id-Fascination (you fascinate me); Orange – Ego-Attention (you have my attention); Blue – Soul-Attention (you are my soul-mate); Violet – Divine Attention (You and I are One).

Octant 2: Cognitive Self in individual relationship as "Your/Thy" Mind. Individual experiential relationship with another.

Octant 3: Inter-Proximate relationship as "You (plural)/Ye" Consciousness. Identification between Selves as a basis for Second Person intimacy.

Octant 4: Cultural Relationship as "Your (plural)" Mind. Relating through sharing experience in the communication of feelings, thoughts, morals and world views.

Octant 5: Distal Persona in individual relationship as "You/Thee" Consciousness. Here is how one sees and evaluates another as an objective identity. After death awareness is of our Non- Local All-Level energy bodies in relationship.

Octant 6: Behavioral Persona in individual relationship as "Your/ Thy" Mind. Relating to the behavior and objectives of another person.

Octant 7: Inter-Objective Relationship as "You (plural)" Consciousness. Socially identifying with others. After death experience is of our relationship in Non-Local All-Level energy environments and realms.

Octant 8: Social Relationship as "Your (plural)" Mind. Shared experience in families, groups, organizations, political parties.

Third Person Pronoun Perspectives

The Third Person is the strongest in Integral Theory, as with the Third Impersonal AQAL Square model and subsequent Eight Fundamental Perspectives. Consequently, it is Integral Theory's greatest endorsement of the AQAL Cube. This is self-evident when differentiating the Eight Fundamental Perspectives both in Third Personal and Third Impersonal perspectives. Third Person Pronoun Perspectives are all about Third Person Consciousness (They/ Their etc). Third Impersonal Pronoun Perspectives of Integral Theory are all about Third Person Energy (It/Its etc).

Octant 1: Phenomenological identity, as "He/She" Consciousness. Identity State-stages as Id, Ego, Soul and Supreme Witness; which correlate with Sub-conscious, Conscious, Super- conscious and Enlightened States; or Gross, Subtle, Causal and Non-Dual experience.

Octant 2: Experiential structures as "His/Her" Mind. The Intelligence Structure-stages of Body- mind, Lower Mind, Higher Mind and Big Mind; which correlate to the fulcrum developmental structures of magic, rational, integral and super-integral/Akashic.

Octant 3: Hermeneutic experience as "They" Consciousness. The Levels of Cultural Identity are according to the capacity to identify, communicate and interpret collective interiors as world views. Representative State-stages are: Red – magical; Orange – scientific-rational; Blue – integral; Violet – post-integral.

Octant 4: Ethnomethodological experience as "Their" Mind. The cultural community where world views take form. Representative Structure-stages are: Red – magical; Orange – scientific- rational; Blue – integral; Violet – post-integral.

Octant 5: Autopoietic experience as "Him/Her" Consciousness. The embedded observer visualizing and imaging through "Inside" processes. As a Non-Local Impersonal entity, the Consciousness monad exists in an Energy body correlating with its Phenomenological level of identity (Octant 1). Representative State-stages are:

Red – Pre-personal; Orange – Ego Persona; Blue – Integrated Persona; Violet – Supra-Personal.

Octant 6: Local processing as "His/Her" Body-Mind. The embodied observer evolving through Levels of increasing physical complexity, through information processing using increasingly fundamental states of energy. Representative Structure-stages are: Red – Limbic/electrochemical; Orange – Neocortex/electromagnetic; Blue – Pineal/quantum; Violet – Supra-pineal/ supraquantum.

Octant 7: Social Autopoietic experience as "Them" Consciousness. The inside agenda of the organizers. As Non-Local Impersonal Realms, they are environments for the Consciousness monad and its Energy Body, as projections in the after-death experience. Representative State- stages are: Red – symbiotic; Orange – server-dominance; Blue – integral; Violet – compassion.

Octant 8: Social Systems experience as "Their" Mind. The arena of organized activity as social environments. Representative Structure-stages: Red – Biosphere; Orange – Noosphere; Blue – Worldsphere; Violet – Theosphere.

REFERENCES

Beck, D
  (1996) *Spiral Dynamics,* Blackwell, Oxford UK
England, J
  (2014) arXiv.org/pdf/1412.1875v1.pdf
Goswami, A
  (1995) *The Self Aware Universe,* Tarcher/Penguin
  (2003) *A Quantum Explanation of Sheldrake's Morphic Resonance*
  Web paper www.stealthskater.com
  (2001) *Physics of the Soul,* Hampton Roads Publishing Company
Hameroff, S
  (2011) *An Exploration of Quantum Consciousness*(Interview),
  EnlighteNext, Issue 46
Haramein, N
  (2004) *The Origin of Spin: A Consideration of Torque and Coriolis
  Forces,* haramein@theresonanceproject.org
  (2008) *Scale Unification,* Unified Theories Conference Proceedings
  (2013) *Quantum Gravity and the Holographic Mass,* Physical Review and Research International
Higgins, C
  (1997) *The Quantum State of Alchemy,* alchemylab.com/quantum1.htm
Hockney, M
  (2014) *The Mathmos* ebook
  (2014) *The Mathematical Universe,* Hyperreality Books
Kurtzweil, R
  (2005) *The Singularity Is Near,* Viking/Penguin, London

Kuypers, W

(2009) *The States and Relevance of Phenomenology for Integral Research,* Integral Review, June vol 5#1

Lao Tzu

Laszlo, E

(2006) *Rationale for an Integral Theory of Everything,* Integral Review, issue #3

(2007) *Science and the Akashic Field,* Inner Traditions, Rochester VT

(2014) *The Primacy of Consciousness, Chapter* contributed to The Re-enchantment of the Cosmos. Inner Traditions, Rochester VT.

Lipton, B

(2005) *The Biology of Belief,* Mountain of Love / Elite Books, Santa Rosa CA

Merry, P

(2012) *petermerry.org/blog/2012/from-evolution-to-volution/*

Neale, L

(2013) *The AQAL Cube for Dummies,* June Issue, Integral Leadership Review

Pali Canon www.palicanon.org

Penrose & Hameroff

(1996) *Towards A Science Of Consciousness,* MIT Press,

Pusey, Barrett, Rudolph

(2011) *On The Reality Of The Quantum State,* arXiv1111.3328.

Radin, D

(2013) www.deanradin.com/papers/Physics%20Radin%20final.pdf

(2013) www.noetic.org/blog/show-me-the-evidence/

Rauscher, E., Amoroso

(2008) Sept.12th. *Relativistic Physics in Complex Minkowsky Space,* Physical Interpretations of Relativity Theory. British Society for Philosophy of Science Conference. Imperial College London

Renshaw, K

(2011) *Why Quantum Entanglement Works,* www.kenrenshaw.com/page6/index.html

Riso, D
(1987, rev 1996) *Personality Types,* Houghton-Mifflin, Boston
Schwartz, G
(2002) *The Afterlife Experiments,* Pocket Books. New York
Secret of the Golden Flower
Anonymous, Traditional
Sheldrake, R
www.sheldrake.org - scientific papers
Sorli, A
(2013) *New horizons of Relativity Theory.* Physics of Now ebook
Stephenson,
(1987) *Children Who Remember Previous Lives,* Charlottesville, University Press of Virgina
Van Lommel, P
(2013). *Journal of Consciousness Studies,* Vol 20, Issue 1/2, p7-48
Wilber, K
(1995) *Sex, Ecology and Spirituality,* Shambhala , Boston
(1996) *Sex, Ecology And Spirituality,* Shambhala, Boston.(p.635)
(2000) *Integral Psychology,* Shambhala, Boston
(2006) *Integral Spirituality,* Integral Books, Boston.
(2009) integrallife.com/video/states-stages-and-3-kinds-self
(2012) *Towards A Comprehensive Theory Of Subtle Energies,* Excerpt G of Vol. 2, The Kosmos Trilogy, kenwilber.com